managing time

Skills in Action

managing time
loving every minute

2nd edition

Peter Green
MA, DipM, MCIM, MCMI, FCIPD

CIM Publishing

CIM Publishing

The Chartered Institute of Marketing
Moor Hall
Cookham
Berkshire
SL6 9QH

www.cim.co.uk

First published 1999
Second edition published 2004
© CIM Publishing 2004

British Library Cataloguing in Publication Data
A CIP catalogue record for this book can be obtained from the British Library.
ISBN 0 902130 65 X

The publishers believe that the contents of this book contribute to debate and offer practical advice. No responsibility will be taken by the publishers for any damage or loss arising from following or interpreting the advice given in this publication.

It is the publisher's policy to use paper manufactured from sustainable forests.

Printed and bound by The Cromwell Press, Trowbridge, Wiltshire.
Cover design by Marcus Andrews.

About the author

Peter Green, a CIM Course Director for many years, has run his own sales and management development consultancy since 1989. Previously he had management experience in sales, personnel, training and marketing services with a multinational market leader.

Independent research has shown the effectiveness of time management training based on his first edition of *Managing Time*. A CIM best-seller, it was published in 1999. This second edition has been extensively updated with new or expanded sections, including decision making, procrastinating and email management.

Acknowledgements

I should like to express my special thanks to:
- Ron Laing and his team at Filofax for their continued book sponsorship and client training opportunities.
- Dr David Green of the University of Central England, Bryan Ruppert and Kevin Hardern of Kevin Hardern Associates for reviewing the draft version and giving constructive feedback from their various academic, linguistic and practitioner perspectives.
- Professor Christina Cavanagh of the University of Western Ontario for access to her research and valuable comments on the email section.
- Dr Denise Skinner and Dr Mark Saunders of Oxford Brookes University for their guidance and encouragement in the design, implementation and analysis of the time management research project.
- The 134 research participants, their managers and training providers for their time and willing co-operation.
- The many writers on time management who have influenced my thinking and practice over the years, especially Alan Lakein, Peter Drucker, Alec Mackenzie, Claus Möller, John Adair, Neil Fiore, Stephen Covey and James Noon.
- John Ling for his editorial skills and encouragement, together with all the CIM external events and training support teams.
- Family, friends, former colleagues, clients and workshop participants from whom I have learnt so much and without whose insights, feedback and encouragement, neither edition of this book would have been possible.

Dedication

To my wife Marion and the important things in life

CONTENTS

Session 7: Personal Action Plan   **155**

Postscript

FOREWORD

Today's world is one of increasing competition, challenge and change. Yet one factor remains constant in our worlds of today, yesterday and yesteryear. Each of us now, as before, only has 1,440 minutes in each day.

As individuals, how we use those precious minutes is now more important than ever if we are to achieve our personal goals in work and life. As organisations, how we use the valuable minutes of our people is even more important if we are to compete on quality, price and productivity in a crowded, global marketplace.

At present, the evidence is that personally and corporately we are not as effective as we might be. Reports of longer working hours, record high levels of workplace stress, and record low levels of workplace loyalty make grim reading. Evidence abounds too of wasted time – with distractions, emails, meetings, cluttered desks, procrastination, lack of planning and poor prioritising.

We are therefore urged to work smarter not harder. The importance of managing our time well is obvious. Yet until now there has been a problem. Whilst we at Filofax have years of anecdotal evidence that our time management training can produce dramatic improvements in people's lives, there has been no reliable, independent evidence that it worked. Indeed, some studies have said time management methods are fine in theory but not in practice.

Happily, we now have that missing proof. Research conducted through Oxford Brookes University of 19 courses based on the first edition of this book showed that participants had an average 20% improvement in personal effectiveness. This was measured after the event by both participants and their managers.

That is why I am especially delighted to continue our sponsorship of Peter Green's book. It is not just theory. It works in practice. It can help you to save time and spend more time on what is important to you. It pulls together the best in time management teaching from across the years. It will help you make the most of your 1,440 minutes each day.

Ron Laing
Managing Director
Filofax UK

Session

1

Session One: Principles

This Session covers seven principles that will affect the way you manage your time:

1. Beware of the "Chicken Farmer Syndrome".
2. Accept your need to change.
3. Unblock your learning.
4. Develop your time management strengths and weaknesses.
5. Manage your mindset.
6. Decide what is important in your life.
7. Balance the imbalances.

1. Beware of the "Chicken Farmer Syndrome"

Reading about this condition will help you appreciate the many references to it throughout the book. Now, I have nothing against chicken farmers; indeed, I used to sell poultry feeds at one time. But I do have concerns about those colleagues of yours who behave like the chicken farmer in the following story...

> 'I'll go and feed the chickens,' said the chicken farmer, picking up his two buckets of grain. Partway across the farmyard, he noticed two roof slates on the ground. 'Oh, I'll put them back on the roof,' said the farmer, putting down his buckets and striding across to the barn for his ladder. 'Oh,' said the farmer, 'the ladder has a rung missing. I'll go and fetch my saw.' And off he went to the tool shed, only to find his saw was rusty. 'Oh dear, I'd better apply some oil,' he said, setting off for the fuel store. 'The oil can is empty. Better get some more from town,' he said, walking towards his Land Rover. When he parked in town, he found he had no money. 'I'll go to the bank,' he said. But in the bank he met a friend, who invited him for a drink... and nobody ever did find out whether the chickens got fed!

> So the Chicken Farmer Syndrome is where the day manages you rather than you manage the day.

You think this a silly story? It is, but there are people who spend their day like this chicken farmer. Perhaps you know some of them. They move on from one unfinished task to another, reacting to every phone call, email, interruption or random thought. So the Chicken Farmer Syndrome is where the day manages you rather than you manage the day. Of course this approach does have its attractions for some people. There is no need to plan or prioritise. They can put off doing difficult tasks. They do not have to think. They only make one decision per day – 'Do I go in today?' Thereafter, the day takes care of itself. The phone rings, a colleague drops by, the boss asks for some figures, a customer has a query, an email arrives, it's time for coffee, there's that meeting to attend, a memo to write, a report to find... Then it's time to go home!

Those friends of yours who are happy with this chicken farmer approach (a reactive mode of underperformance and missed deadlines) we can only leave to their fate. For your other chicken farmer friends who want to plan, prioritise and take more control of their time and their lives, the following pages provide plenty of ideas.

2. Accept your need to change

The Los Angeles Police Department are credited with the slogan 'If you always do what you've always done, you'll always get what you've always got!' Alas, this slogan also applies to how you manage your time. Unless you are deliriously happy with your time management, you will have to make changes, and changes mean doing some things differently. Try this exercise...

> 'If you always do what you've always done, you'll always get what you've always got!'

When no one is looking, clasp your hands together. Look down at your hands and see which thumb is on top. Now unclasp you hands and put them together again with the other thumb on top.

You can hardly call the movement difficult, but the result does feel **different.** Similarly, the principles, guidelines, ideas and techniques in this book are not difficult, but they may be different to your current practices. For you to improve your time management you will need to do some things differently, try new ideas, and change the status quo. Otherwise the time problems you have when you finish this book will be exactly the same as those you had when you started.

3. Unblock your learning

90% of the 250 companies involved in CIM's Training Survey (2002) identified the transfer of learning within an organisation as an increasingly important issue. Encouragingly, the learning transfer from 19 training courses based on this book was significant. The courses produced an average 20% improvement in personal effectiveness some three months after the training. This was measured by the participants themselves and verified by their managers in research conducted through Oxford Brookes University.

That is the good news. The bad news is that individual responses varied widely from minus 10% to plus 141%! This wide variation is consistent with numerous research papers discussing personal, psychological and organisational barriers that get in the way of our learning. Drawn from a variety of these sources, 16 of the most common factors are shown in Figure 1.

Non-training influences affecting training outcomes

Impedes Learning	Factor	Helps Learning
	PERSONAL	
Poor	Health	Good
Failing	Relationships	Thriving
High	Stress	Low
Out of control	Finance	Under control
	PSYCHOLOGICAL	
Low	Perceived Employability	High
Low	Self-esteem	High
Ineffective	Assertiveness	Effective
Low	Motivation to Learn	High
Luck, fate, others	Responsibility for Results	Me
	ORGANISATIONAL	
Mainly reactive	Job Role	Mainly proactive
Low involvement	Learning & Job Decisions	High involvement
No or few opportunities	Applying the Learning	Lots of opportunities
Unsupportive	The Boss	Supportive
Unco-operative	Colleagues	Co-operative
Inadequate	Resources to do the Job	Adequate
The hours you put in	Culture Focus	What you put in the hours

Figure 1

Hopefully, none of these issues will be a problem to you, in which case go straight to the **New Ideas Exercise.** However, should one or two of them relate to your situation, here are some suggested strategies to remove these blocks and maximise your learning.

Personal: Depending upon how serious the personal problem is, either seek professional help or focus on the potential benefits to you of improved time management. One of the benefits is a greater feeling of being in control in a changing world, with the potential to help you improve your health, stress and general well-being. Whilst effective time management is no panacea, it is a life skill that will repay the removal of any personal blocks to learning about it.

Psychological: Your employability and self-esteem will both improve if you adopt some of the simple, research-proven techniques and ideas contained in this book. Later on we will discuss the benefits of being more assertive, as opposed to non-assertive or aggressive behaviour. You can use these skills to enrich your personal as well as working life, and they are fully transferable from one job to another. Also, according to research, the greater responsibility you take for what you do, rather than blaming fate or other people, the more likely you are to learn and profit from your learning.

Organisational: Job roles can be considered from a reactive versus proactive perspective. By reactive I mean responding to a situation rather than creating or controlling it. As we will see in the next Session, we all need to be reactive to events to some extent. However, some jobs are obviously more reactive than others. An Accident and Emergency surgeon, a computer helpline specialist, and a call-centre operative all have more reactive jobs than, say, a business strategist. The perception that a job is reactive and therefore planning is impossible can be a barrier to learning for some. It is certainly true that the more reactive the role, the less opportunity there will be to implement some of the time management techniques we discuss. However, it is also arguably true that the more reactive your job, the more important it is to make sound use of whatever discretionary time you do have. I will show you how to do this later.

If any of the other organisational factors are a problem, I would suggest you proactively seek a meeting with your line manager after you have read the book. List the new ideas you would like to adopt and highlight the potential benefits not only for yourself but also for your manager. Ask for their support and try to influence such things as organisational culture if this is an issue. In the unlikely event of your failing to get this support, my favourite word is "despite". Despite this and that problem, you can still achieve more in less time with less stress, provided you have a positive "can do" mindset. So unblock your learning and keep an open mind on new ideas.

New Ideas Exercise

If you have come across this exercise before – beware! There are variants about. Anyway, read the following section carefully and count the number of letter F's in it.

> **FINISHED FILES ARE THE RESULT**
> **OF YEARS OF SCIENTIFIC**
> **STUDY COMBINED WITH THE**
> **EXPERIENCE OF MANY YEARS.**

Your Answer: __ (To be absolutely sure, check it once more).

Now, you are perfectly capable of identifying how many F's there are in a sentence, just as you are perfectly capable of identifying a good idea when you see one. The odd thing is, however, that when people first do this exercise, their answers usually vary between three and six. Indeed, if you saw fewer than six, have another check. If you are still in doubt, count the number of times the word "of" appears.

The point of the exercise is to show how we can look at something, such as a sentence or a time management idea, and believe we can see what is there. But we might be missing something. We might dismiss an idea as a "3F" idea, whereas in reality, it might be a "6F" idea and well worth our while trying. If this exercise encourages you to keep an open mind on all the ideas that follow, it will achieve its aim, as well as providing some potential after-dinner entertainment!

4. Develop your time management strengths and weaknesses

Is it in the genes? Is your ability to manage your time a question of personality, temperament or innate ability? Before we get into another nature versus nurture debate, I will come down unequivocally on the sides of "yes" and "no"! Yes, we are born with different personalities and motivations that affect our time management behaviours. And no, we cannot hide behind these because all of us are capable of building on our strengths and overcoming our weaknesses.

Personality traits themselves can be measured in several ways, using various psychometric tests or instruments. These can range from the simple, one-dimensional Type A/B test we will look at in a moment, to the more sophisticated, multi-dimensional models such as the well-known Myers-Briggs Type Indicator® , and my personal favourite, the Strength Deployment Inventory®
(see www.personalstrengths.co.uk for more details).

All these measures have a common message – the behavioural traits we have will affect our instinctive approach to the way we manage our time. For all of us, some of these ways are effective whilst others are not. The better we know ourselves, the better able we will be to build on our time management strengths and work on improving our inherent weaknesses. Let us illustrate this with a simple example, focusing on one specific behavioural scale – dominance.

Dominance Exercise

Low Dominance   1 2 3 4 5   High Dominance

In the table below, circle the number which most accurately describes the degree to which others perceive you as wanting to control the thoughts and actions of others. What natural tendencies do you display in your behaviour?

Unassuming	1 2 3 4 5	Bold
Quiet	1 2 3 4 5	Talkative
Accepting	1 2 3 4 5	Challenging
Reserved	1 2 3 4 5	Forceful
Cautious	1 2 3 4 5	Outgoing
Asks	1 2 3 4 5	Tells
Takes time to act	1 2 3 4 5	Swift to act
Thoughtful decisions	1 2 3 4 5	Quick decisions
Supportive	1 2 3 4 5	Directive
Less confrontational	1 2 3 4 5	More confrontational

Add up your scores and divide the total by 10. This will give you a score of between 1 and 5. There is no right or wrong score. Irrespective of where your score lies, you can be a highly effective manager of your time.

The nearer your score is to 1, the more of a "Type B", low dominance person you are. The nearer your score is to 5, the more of a "Type A", high dominance person you are.

Whichever type you are, you should be aware of the potential dangers you need to guard against. For instance:

Type B/low dominant people often have a calm approach to life, working at an unhurried pace. They tend to be organised and methodical, have an eye for detail, and are more concerned about quality than quantity. In consequence, they can sometimes set unrealistically high standards of quality for a task and unrealistically low standards of output.

Type A/high dominant people on the other hand are usually action driven. They focus on results rather than methods, and can be perceived as aggressive, competitive and "busy". As a result, they can sometimes find it difficult to say "no", take on unrealistic workloads, be weak on planning and prioritising, and sometimes cause "people problems".

Thus both Type A and Type B people have in-built strengths and weaknesses. To be really effective managers of their time, both need to build on their strengths and work on their weaknesses. A small team I saw in action highlighted this. The Sales Director was a Type A, all-action man, constantly pushing his two Type B Research Assistants to get new products out to the sales team faster, so as to beat the competition. He was exasperated with their insistence on detail and failure to act quickly enough. 'They are perfectionists,' he complained, 'and as Winston Churchill once said, the word perfection spells P-a-r-a-l-y-s-i-s'. For their part, the Researchers were riled by the Director's lack of planning. 'He wants us to sell the product when it is not in the warehouse, not on the order form, and hasn't been priced yet,' they bemoaned. Attention to detail and being action-oriented are both strengths. Yet when they are overdone, the strengths become weaknesses. The Type A Director had to learn to plan a bit more, and the Type B Researchers had to learn to be less perfectionist, if they were to achieve their mutual goal of successful product launches. Similarly, all of us need to build on our time management strengths, but be aware of and improve our time management weaknesses, if we are to achieve what we want to achieve.

5. Manage your mindset

Are you the victim of the "Don Quixote Syndrome", "Parkinson's Law", or "Faulty Time Norms"? All of these are defective mindsets that can eat up needless hours of your time and energy. Taking each in turn, we begin with the Don Quixote Syndrome, named after the famously naïve, unworldly and idealistic seventeenth-century Cervantes character, who sought to fight windmills, believing they were giants. Alas, his followers live on in the twenty-first century and here are two real-life examples.

The Don Quixote Syndrome

Roger's company had to cut costs and decided to give everyone smaller company cars. No one liked it, but it did cut costs and did make sense. It was also a fait accompli that was not going to change, so everyone quickly came to terms with it and got on with life. Everyone that is except Roger. Roger's fury lasted not days, not weeks, not even months, but literally two to three years. It was clearly eating away inside him, as the most innocent of comments could spark an eruption of emotion and diatribe on company car policy, which, as everyone else knew, was always going to fall on deaf ears.

Michelle and Raj were both business advisors with a government quango, or quasi-autonomous non-governmental organisation. Michelle was regularly incensed and frustrated by the lack of a common policy between similar quangos, excessive paperwork, appalling bureaucracy, and the convoluted process her client companies had to go through to qualify for financial support. Raj nodded and agreed, but had a different approach. 'There is no point getting wound up about it,' he told a client. 'That is the way it is. If by hopping on one leg for two minutes you would qualify for a substantial business grant would you do it?' 'Of course' said the client. 'Well, we don't want you to hop, but you will have to go along with a less than perfect system if you want the money. Let's accept the imperfections and get on with it.'

Raj was a pragmatist who accepted the bureaucracy as a fact of life that wasn't going to change, so spent his time and effort working within the system. By contrast, Roger and Michelle were latter-day Don Quixotes, using up their finite time and energy in battles they could never win. They offer a warning to us all to make sure we are spending our precious time on worthwhile ventures.

Parkinson's Law

Tongue-in-cheek though it may have been, there is much truth in Cyril Northcote Parkinson's satirical dictum that **'Work expands to fill the time available for its completion'.**

For instance, I know of one department in a particular company that had a reputation for being a really committed, hard-working group of people. They rarely went home before 7pm, usually 8pm, and sometimes not until 9pm. It was their norm. It was what they did. The job demanded it. They accepted it. The cracks in this argument first appeared when reports came back from people in other departments who had to work an occasional late stint. 'Yes these people work late,' they all agreed, 'but they don't seem to be working hard.' Further investigations showed that this was classic Parkinson's Law. They all had a mindset which said we work until 7 or 8pm and that is how long our work will take us. But when their new director insisted that they left at a sensible hour, despite their protestations, he proved conclusively that their work could be done in much less time.

Similarly, I frequently hear of women returning from maternity leave achieving as much as they ever did, even though they now have to leave on time for their baby-minder. I also know of an academic who decided to leave on time every Tuesday and Thursday, come what may. 'Sorry, I have to leave now,' he would say, even in the middle of a meeting. The fact that he was off to the pub quiz night on Tuesdays and a gym session on Thursdays was incidental. It enabled him to break his long-hours mindset and he has since seen his career flourish.

Sometimes then, the reason people work long hours is of their own making, though in some cases it is more to do with an organisation's long-hours culture (this will be discussed in Session Five).

Faulty Time Norms

So, staying with personal rather than organisational issues, many people can be said to have faulty time norms in terms of how much time is needed for certain jobs. Here are some more "fault lines".

> There were two animal feeds salesmen on adjacent territories. One was convinced he could not start early until after his farmers had had their breakfasts. But he could work late when the farmers were milking their cows and were a captive audience. The other salesmen knew he could call early on farmers when they were having their breakfast as they were at home then and not out in the fields. But he was convinced that he had to finish early before milking, as no one would want to see him then.

Two salesmen with their own idea of what the "norm" was and what could and could not be done. And they each proved the other wrong. I know – I was one of those salesmen! I had a faulty mindset. Do you?

Mindset Review

Are **you** fighting any windmills? Are **you** a victim of Parkinson's Law? Do **you** have any faulty time norms?	
If "yes", what are you going to do about it?	

6. Decide what is important in your life

'UK workers struggle to balance work and quality of life as long hours and stress take hold.' So say the Department of Trade and Industry (DTI). The DTI were so concerned about the adverse effect this was having on the UK's ability to compete in world markets, that in 2000 they launched a national Work-Life Balance Campaign. Whilst work-life balance means different things to different people, the DTI believes it is about adjusting working patterns to help people combine work with their other responsibilities and aspirations.

Personal work-life balance issues are covered in Session Four whilst organisational ones are covered in Session Five. For the moment, we will focus on the balance itself, by helping you review what is really important to you. So, before we go into the micro nuts and bolts of time management, let us in this section at least, take a macro "helicopter view" and ask a question: how do you really want to spend your time and your life? Before answering, put your thoughts into context by considering the rapidly changing world in which we live.

> Work-life balance is about adjusting working patterns to help people combine work with their other responsibilities and aspirations.

Industry changes: 'During the early 1900s, 70% of UK workers were in agriculture. Now agriculture involves less than 2% of the workforce.' Price Pritchett, *New Work Habits for a Radically Changing World.*

Information overload: 'The amount of information generated has grown about 30% every year since 1999.' Prof. Peter Lyman, University of California/BBC News, November 2003.

Computer development: 'There is a world market for about five computers.' Thomas J. Watson, founder of IBM, 1943.

Internet development: 'The World Wide Web was only introduced in 1991. By 2001 there were an estimated 450 million regular users of the Internet. By 2005, this is forecast to be 2 billion.' *Key UK Trends: 2001-2011.* Cabinet Office, 2003.

Mobile phones: 'Introduced in 1985, the first generation of analogue phones weighed around 5kg, cost several thousand pounds, and had a battery life of less than a day. The second generation of digital phones now owned by 75% of the UK population can weigh only 60g, cost nothing, and have a battery life of up to ten days.' *Oftel, 2002.*

Job patterns: 'Whilst work will continue to be intrinsically interesting for some, for others it is increasingly becoming a means to an end, rather than an end in itself, with fun, leisure and personal fulfilment being the primary end.' Futurist, March-April 2001.

Family life: 'The number of men and women between 24 and 44 living alone is six times greater than 30 years ago.' General Household Survey, 2004.

Professional knowledge: 'Now, the "shelf-life" of professional knowledge is down to five years, or less in many areas, and is shrinking. In the world of information technology it is already down to a year or less.' Mark Whitehead, *Marketing Business, October 1998.*

Times change – but basic human needs do not. This has implications for how we spend our time. One way of looking at this is to consider the basic needs we all have, as expressed in Abraham Maslow's long-established model. He saw human needs in a hierarchy, the lower ones needing to be satisfied first, before we move on to the higher ones (Figure 2).

Maslow's hierarchy of human needs

Physiological	Safety	Social	Esteem	Self-actualisation
				(Later redefined as: Living for a purpose higher than self.)
			Self-respect Status. Recognition.	
		Belonging. Love. Social activities.		
	Security. Protection from danger.			Personal development. Accomplish-ment.
Hunger. Thirst. Sleep.				

Figure 2

In the past, the means to satisfy the physiological and safety needs were met by the income obtained from employment. In today's world employment is much less certain than it used to be. There are no longer "jobs for life", but there is "learning for life". If we want to cope with a rapidly changing world, where some jobs will disappear or be drastically reduced, and other as yet undreamed of jobs will appear, we need to keep learning. Continuing Professional Development (CPD) is here to stay and we need to make adequate time for it.

To meet our social and esteem needs, we need to interact effectively with other people. So how important to you are a partner, children, family, friends or community? If they are important, how will you show this in terms of the time you commit to them?

When other needs are met, our highest need says Maslow, is to reach our full potential. And we can only do that, he finally concludes, by looking outwards to the needs of others, rather than just looking inwards to our own needs. Remember the famous epitaph to Sir Christopher Wren in St Paul's Cathedral, 'If you seek his monument, look around you.' What monument you leave behind will depend upon what things you consider to be important, and how much time you consequently invest in them.

Importance Exercise

To help you focus on what is important in your life, here is a short, three-part exercise.

Part 1 – Where you are now

Reflect on your level of satisfaction in the various aspects of your life listed. Taken together, they will cover your needs according to Maslow's model. They offer the means to put a roof over your head and food on the table, build rewarding relationships, nurture a good self-image, and provide opportunities to develop your full potential.

✓ – Aspects you are content with. × – Aspects that you need to do something about.
✳ – Aspects you are currently working on.
In the space provided, write down any objectives that you want to achieve.

✓	LIFE ASPECT	COMMENTS/AIMS
	1. FINANCIAL	
	• Income level	
	• Property	
	• Pension	
	• Savings and investments	
	2. CAREER	
	• Qualifications and competencies	
	• Continuing Professional Development	
	• Achievement of results	
	• Readiness for promotion	
	3. SPIRITUAL	
	• Personal beliefs and values	
	• Understanding oneself and others	
	• Developing quality relationships	
	• Giving as well as receiving	
	4. SOCIAL	
	• Significant other	
	• Family	
	• Friends	
	• Community involvement	
	5. CULTURAL	
	• Performing and visual arts	
	• Reading	
	• Further education	
	• Hobbies and interests	
	6. HEALTH	
	• Fitness and exercise	
	• Sports	
	• Lifestyle	
	• Coping with stress	

Part 2 – Where you want to be

Jot down in the first column what you want to have, be or do, based on your thoughts in Part 1. In the next column, write down what this means you need to do.

I want to have, be or do:	Which means that I need to:
1. FINANCIAL	
2. CAREER	
3. SPIRITUAL	
4. SOCIAL	
5. CULTURAL	
6. HEALTH	

Part 3 – How you are going to get there

List the four to five most important objectives you would like to achieve (we will return to these in the next Session.) Before doing so, reconcile any conflicts in Part 2 and ensure that you are prepared to "pick up the tab" and pay the price of the consequences of your aims.

For instance, if you want to become a chief executive, are you prepared to put in the extra effort, and possibly hours, to get there? Will this commitment be at an acceptable level for your family and social life? Will it bring happiness as well as success?

'Success is getting what you want. Happiness is liking what you get.' H. Jackson Brown

Having reflected on all this, now list your objectives.

My Top Personal Objectives are...

1.

2.

3.

4.

5.

7. Balance the imbalances

Even when we have decided what is important to us, we can still suffer from conflicting demands on our time. Usually these come under one of five headings:

1. **Short term, event linked** e.g. year-end budget, national conference, product launch, stocktaking, an illness, or the arrival of a baby.
2. **Medium term, life-stage linked** e.g. studying for a qualification, looking after young children/elderly relatives, or extra work to build a career.
3. **One-off conflicts** e.g. being late for your partner's solo in a concert because of an accident on the motorway.
4. **Chronic imbalances** e.g. persistently missing children's school events, or excessive time in a sport, work, hobby or interest to the detriment of the family or a relationship.
5. **Comfort zone imbalances** e.g. when promoted, spending too much time doing familiar technical/operational work rather than the unfamiliar management work.

With good communication, agreement and mutual understanding, the first three types can usually be overcome by taking a longer-term view of aiming to "balance the imbalances". For instance, if you have had heavy involvement in a project (be it work or community related) for a couple of months, you can perhaps balance this with a long weekend away, taking time to refresh yourself and your relationship.

> 'Success is getting what you want. Happiness is liking what you get.'
>
> H. Jackson Brown

Chronic work-life imbalances, however, suggest a need to review again just what is important in your life. It is better to do this proactively than let it happen to you with one of life's "wake-up calls", e.g. a serious illness or tragic accident. Such an occurrence often forces us to reflect on our personal Richter scale. At these times we often get a much clearer picture of what **really** is important. Good time managers, and good life managers, practise preventative medicine by spotting chronic imbalances, discussing them with friends or their significant other, and agreeing the best solution.

As for comfort-zone imbalances, this is a challenge all of us face throughout our careers. As Figure 3 demonstrates, as we climb the management ladder we should be spending less of our time "doing" the technical side of our work, and more of our time "managing". Technical work can be defined as work specific to a particular function, such as accounting, marketing or distribution. Management work, on the other hand, is common to all functions; examples being planning, organising, leading and controlling. In practice, many managers, especially those newly promoted, tend to hang on to their technical work. It is what they know. It is usually what they are good at. It is their comfort zone. Some find it difficult to let go and delegate some of this work. In which case, the only way they can carry out their management role as well is to work longer hours. They need to learn to delegate effectively and this skill will be covered later in Session Five.

Management time

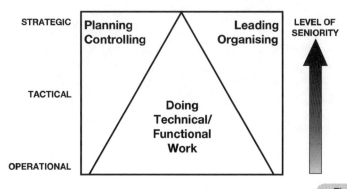

Figure 3

However, whilst delegating technical work is vital for any manager, I am not suggesting that they never get their hands dirty. All managers need to roll up their sleeves at times, lead by example, and do some of the "doing" work. So constantly check your managing/doing allocation of time. Are you well balanced?

SUMMARY OF SESSION ONE: Principles

1. Manage the day, don't let the day manage you.
2. Accept the need to change your time management. **'If you always do what you've always done, you'll always get what you've always got.'**
3. Unblock your learning by tackling any personal, psychological or organisational barriers.
4. Know your innate time management strengths and weaknesses and work on both.
5. Beware of defective mindsets, such as the Don Quixote Syndrome, Parkinson's Law and Faulty Time Norms.
6. Decide what is **really important** in your life and be prepared to pay the price.
7. Keep balancing any short-term and long-term work-life imbalances and any managing-doing imbalances.

Session

2

Session Two: Planning Ahead

From general principles, we now turn to specific aspects of managing your time. Whilst the focus is workplace oriented, the ideas can also be applied to many home and non-work situations. In this Session we will look at:

1. Direction – are you full-steam adrift?
2. Key Result Areas – what are yours?
3. Goals – in the absence of clairvoyants get SMARTER.
4. Action plans – be start-line focused.
5. Diary management and the cure for "cancelitis".
6. Schedules and time frames – get real!
7. Monitoring – goodbye to control freaks and metal coffins!
8. Personal planning – is there life after work?

1. Direction – are you full-steam adrift?

Later in this and further Sessions, we will look at how to set medium-term goals and how to plan, prioritise and schedule these into daily activities – the "clock" part of the process. But how can we possibly prioritise effectively if we do not know where we are going and what we are trying to achieve? For this we need some form of "compass".

Vision to action cycle

Mission Statement
↓
Business Plan
↓
Key Result Area
↓
Individual Objective
↓
Prioritising the Day
↓
Performance Review
↓
Training Plan

Figure 4

Everybody knows organisations that keep moving the goal posts. Sometimes they move the playing field as well – without telling anyone! This creates frustration and we can often observe the phenomenon of "full-steam adrift". Everyone is rushing energetically and with good intentions, but people are rarely travelling in the same direction.

Yet based on the UK Investors in People standard of best practice, everyone in an organisation should have a shared picture of what the organisation is trying to do, where it is going, and how an individual's particular job contributes to this (Figure 4).

Effective companies achieve this by producing a Mission Statement based on a vision of the future and on the values that the company will reflect in its dealings. The vision and values become the organisation's compass bearing. In a changing world and changing markets, it provides guidance on what is important.

The Mission Statement should, therefore, influence the content of the annual, flexible business plan. What are we going to do this year to make our Mission more of a reality? In the next three sections of this Session, we will explore the link between business plan, Key Result Areas, department objectives and individual objectives. Then in Session Three we will link these objectives to daily planning and prioritising.

For now, let us assess how you and your organisation rate at compass reading. If there are any grey areas about what is expected of you, proactively seek clarification from your manager.

Personal Checklist Exercise

	Yes	No
Does your organisation have a Mission Statement?	❑	❑
Does your organisation have a business plan?	❑	❑
Do you know the broad goals and content of the business plan?	❑	❑
Do you know how your job will help the organisation achieve it?	❑	❑
Do you have clear performance standards and agreed objectives?	❑	❑
Are there any aspects of your job that you need to clarify with your manager?	❑	❑

Notes

2. Key Result Areas – what are yours?

In Figure 4, we saw that an individual employee's objectives should ideally be clearly linked to achieving the business plan and ultimately the organisation's mission. An increasing number of organisations are making this connection by means of the Balanced Scorecard approach devised by Professor Robert Kaplan and Dr David Norton at the Harvard Business School. This provides a framework of goals and measures from four perspectives – financial, internal process development, customers and innovation and learning. Other organisations prefer to use Key Performance Indicators (KPIs) to link their business plan to an individual's expected contribution and objectives. Making that link is more important than which method is used.

The method we will use here to help make the mission happen is by mapping out the Key Result Areas (KRAs) of the organisation down to individual level. For instance, the KRAs of a furniture manufacturer might be marketing, production, finance, distribution and sales. Each of these areas has to be effective if the company is to be successful, and each of these disciplines has its own KRAs.

A sales director's might be domestic sales, export sales, key customers, new business, sales budgets, market intelligence and personnel and training.

Objectives can be set in each of these key areas, both to maintain the business and to improve it. Alas, directors cannot achieve all these objectives by themselves! They need ordinary mortals to help them. They need to set targets, performance standards and objectives for each individual. This is made easier if each person has KRAs. It makes sure that important parts of the business are not overlooked.

The benefit of KRAs for the individual is that they help to keep an overview of what the job is really about. They are a defence mechanism against being drowned in day-to-day detail and help people to separate the wood from the trees.

How do you decide what your Key Result Areas are? Here are some guidelines:

1. Research suggests that the subconscious brain can cope with about seven headings. In practice a minimum of four and maximum of seven works well.
2. If you come up with more than seven – cheat! Amalgamate one or two headings. For instance "Internal Contacts" and "External Contacts" could be listed as subheadings under a main heading of "Contacts" or "Communications".
3. Keep your headings brief. They should be convenient memory pegs on which to hang all the parts of your job.
4. Two people doing the same job may come up with different headings. There is no single correct way. As long as the headings make sense to you and provide an umbrella under which each of your activities can sit they are fine.

Here are two examples of Key Result Areas in addition to those of the sales director listed earlier:

Sales Executive
1. Communications
2. Customers
3. Prospects
4. Call preparation
5. Product and market information
6. Sales figures and targets
7. Personal development

Marketing Manager
1. Market research
2. Product portfolio
3. Product development
   - New products
   - Product launch schedule
4. Sales and budgets
5. Advertising and PR
6. Training and development
7. Communications
   - Internal
   - External

Key Result Areas Exercise

Now it's your turn! What are the Key Result Areas for your job? Use the grid below. Use pencil so that you can easily modify your first attempt if necessary. Later in the Session, we can set objectives for the things you want to achieve in some or all of your Key Result Areas.

My Key Areas

1.	
2.	
3.	
4.	
5.	
6.	
7.	

3. Goals – in the absence of clairvoyants get SMARTER

Humour me for a moment; draw a line in the rectangle below.

Based on past experience, I am not at all confident that you have done what I wanted. Having seen various people try this exercise on training courses over many years, I have come to the depressing conclusion that there is a national, nay, worldwide shortage of clairvoyants.

Whilst I know exactly what I want, other people do not seem to have a clue. For instance, in the exercise above, I wanted a vertical line, two centimetres long, one centimetre from the top of the box, three centimetres from the left-hand side, dotted and in red felt tip. But is that what you gave me? Now do you believe in the lack of clairvoyants? This has serious implications for the effective use of your time. Remember: 'If you don't know where you are going, you will end up somewhere else.' Laurence J Peter.

> 'If you don't know where you are going, you will end up somewhere else.'
>
> Laurence J Peter.

This exercise simply underlines that. Unless you spell out what you want very clearly, you do not have an objectives list, you have a wish list. You may have good intentions to make things happen, but the odds are they will only be as successful as the typical New Year's resolution. You are in grave danger of wasting your time and the time of any others you embroil in your vague notions. Remember that the more clearly you define what you want, the more likely you are to achieve it.

The traditional SMART acronym requires an objective to be Specific, Measurable, Agreed, Realistic and Time-bound. The SMARTER objective (Figure 5), adds Evaluated – actual results checked against planned results to assess the need for corrective action; and Reviewed – was the objective achieved and what can we all learn from the experience?

SMARTER objectives

S **pecific** – quantified and clear, not vague.

M **easurable** – how will you do this?

A **greed** – better to involve than impose.

R **ealistic** – achievable but stretching.

T **imed** – with a time frame and deadline.

E **valuated** – check progress against the plan.

R **eviewed** – what can we learn?

Figure 5

By setting ourselves SMARTER objectives, we are much more likely to achieve the results we desire. Setting vague objectives like "draw a line" will only end in tears. There is one exception. If senior management sets vague objectives, they are then called strategic or high-level objectives! In fairness, this is usually quite legitimate, provided assistance in clarifying the vagueness is forthcoming from them.

For instance, what do you make of one company's objective, which was 'To enter the chilled and frozen foods market'? It is clearly not SMART, having no measurables such as monetary or unit values, no target market sectors, and no timescale – to name but a few shortcomings! It did, though, spell out the board's strategic intent to seek pastures new. This is sufficient for high-level business planning purposes, but certainly insufficient for the project leader.

Having established the general aim, the company then asked for research to be conducted into what the project would involve, and for detailed proposals to be submitted. As a result a SMARTER objective was then written with more detail. Changing the numbers this became 'To achieve £2 million of chilled and frozen sales, at 4% net profit, by the end of the next financial year, by means of telephone and direct sales through our existing distribution channels.'

If you want labels to differentiate between these higher and lower-level objectives, try "goals or aims" for the former, and "objectives or targets" for the latter. 'Are these universally recognised in all organisations?' you might ask. If only! Attempts have been made to agree a common management vocabulary, but to no avail. Just be aware of the different levels of objectives and the fairly casual, interchangeable usage in some companies of words like goals, aims, objectives, budgets and targets.

Above all, ensure that when you accept or set objectives, everyone involved is absolutely agreed on what a successful outcome will be.

Having looked at the theory, we now come to the practice. Can you spot and write SMARTER objectives? This is an important management skill which can save you and your colleagues hours of wasted time.

Spot The Smarter Objective

Which of the following objectives do you consider to be SMARTER? Bullet point your comments under each one and compare them with those given at the end of this Session.

1. To increase sales by 10%.

2. To launch Product X by the end of the second quarter.

3. To improve the credit position from 82 days to 60 days by the end of the financial year and maintain it at or below that level thereafter.

4. To improve the performance of the retail sales force by:

   - Increasing their calls per day.
   - Reducing their miles per call.
   - Better prospecting.

5. To identify a suitable venue for the 2006 spring exhibition which:

   - Has good road and rail links.
   - Projects a professional image.
   - Will keep within budget.
   - Has a suitable room.
   - Is available for three days in the second week of March.

Here are some guidelines for writing SMARTER objectives:

1. **Write the objective first, *then* check to see if it is SMART.**
   Do not start with something Specific, then something Measurable etc. It does not work that way.
2. **Keep action steps for the action plans.**
   It is usually easier to keep the objective (**what** you are doing) separate from the action steps (**how** you are doing it).

3. **Consider listing the success criteria.**
   For example, in the "draw a line" exercise, the success criteria were that the line should be vertical, two centimetres long, one centimetre from the top, three centimetres from the left-hand side, dotted, and in red felt tip. This success criteria approach is especially useful for some bigger, more complex objectives.

4. **Remember that some measurable criteria are numbers such as £, profit, % increase or units sold, whilst others are simply measured by a "yes" or "no".**
   Back to our "draw a line" example. The length and position can be checked in units (centimetres in this case). Whether the line was vertical, dotted and done in red felt tip can be checked with a straight "yes" or "no".

5. **If some aspects of what you are trying to do are to be determined later, perhaps after some research, the word "agreed" is often useful.**
   'To launch the product at an agreed date' is not a cop-out. It requires you to determine who you need to agree the date with at some time before the launch, and thereafter it is measurable.

6. **Try the Colleague Clarity Test.**
   Show your completed objective to a colleague and go through the SMARTER checklist together. If it makes sense to both of you, you are probably on the right lines.

7. **Try the Ultimate Test.**
   If you can write objectives for yourself and your people that are consistently easy to understand, monitor and review, and they deliver the results you want, you are certainly writing SMARTER objectives. You are also certainly saving your (and everyone else's) precious time!

Objectives Exercise

Write a SMARTER objective for something that you want to achieve in one of your Key Result Areas (Page 21). Similarly, write an objective linked to one of your personal aims (Page 14). Pick something that is worth your while doing that you have not already planned. That way it becomes a practical, worthwhile exercise. We will come back to this later in the Session.

Business objective:

Personal objective:

4. Action plans – be start-line focused

In our planning so far, we have determined our general direction, the key areas that will generate results, and one or two objectives that we want to achieve. We now turn to how we can make things happen. How do we turn our vision into action, our dreams into reality? There are two main approaches, deadline focused and start-line focused. Here is how they work.

The deadline-focused approach (Figure 6) has you coming out of your boss's office breathing a great sigh of relief that, thank heavens, you have (say) six months to achieve the objective she has just set you. So we can forget about that for the moment and concentrate on all the other things you have to do right now.

Deadline-focused projects

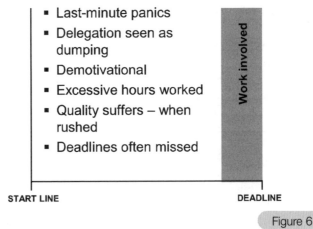

- Last-minute panics
- Delegation seen as dumping
- Demotivational
- Excessive hours worked
- Quality suffers – when rushed
- Deadlines often missed

Work involved

START LINE   DEADLINE

Figure 6

Then coming up to the deadline, a chance comment or sight of a document reminds you that you now have only (say) a couple of weeks to achieve what you promised. Panic! Have you seen the amount of work you have to do on this? Oh dear! That is the weekend taken care of and you will have to work late each night if you are to have any hope of... now wait a minute: you went on a training course, didn't you? And what was that word they used? Yes, that's the one – delegation! Great! (If you have no one to delegate to, sorry, but you are in serious trouble!)

So you now rush round your people, telling them to stop whatever they are doing because this is **urgent!** 'Sorry about the extra workload but needs must.' 'Teamwork.' 'All pull together.' 'We can do it', and similar cheery comments.

> Taking a deadline-focused approach to achieving objectives or managing projects is very good if you want to work extra-long hours at a frantic rate, upset your staff, produce rushed work, and risk missing the deadline anyway!

Unfortunately your people do not tend to see it as delegating but as dumping! I call it "Friday Afternoon Syndrome". You are just looking forward to a relaxing, enjoyable weekend, when work arrives from the boss that must be ready for Monday. You are loyal, so do it, but you cannot help but wonder how long this job has been in your boss's in-tray.

Taking a deadline-focused approach to achieving objectives or managing projects is very good if you want to work extra-long hours at a frantic rate, upset your staff, produce rushed work, and risk missing the deadline anyway!

There is an alternative. It is the start-line-focused approach, which, surprisingly, starts at the start (Figure 7). With this approach, you come out of your boss's office with your six-month deadline and immediately go into action plan mode. OK! If we want to achieve this objective by the deadline, what are the key milestones along the way? Who will have to do what by when if we are to get there in time?

Rather than have one big last minute panic, this approach offers you a series of mini-panics as you come to each milestone! If you miss one, it is not the end of the world – you still have time to catch up before the next milestone. You have a built-in control mechanism to compare your planned-versus-actual progress.

You spread the workload and thereby increase the likelihood of producing quality work on time. It is less exciting than the deadline approach, but it is also less stressful! It also gives the opportunity to involve your colleagues from the outset, so they know the timescale and "own" the delivery as much as you do.

Start-line-focused projects

- Immediate action plan
- Milestones with mini-deadlines
- Spreads the workload with less stress
- Quality and achievement benefits

Work involved

START LINE   DEADLINE

Figure 7

5. Diary management and the cure for "cancelitis"

Another effect of being deadline-focused is the predisposition to the condition I call "cancelitis". You have probably heard this typical conversation:

> Yes I know the course/meeting/visit has been in the diary for two months, but well, I have this very important project and sorry – but I really will have to cancel. I have spoken to my boss who agrees that completing the project is much more important than the course/meeting/visit. So I'm afraid I won't be there.

So often with persistent offenders, this tendency to cancel or change plans at the last minute is hugely predictable. It is just symptomatic of poor diary planning. The project's deadline has often been known as long as the date of the event they are cancelling. But unless the person becomes start-line focused and spreads the workload, pressures will always arise nearing deadlines, increasing the likelihood of having to cancel everything else.

Apart from sound planning, what is needed is good diary management.
Let us test this out.

Diary Exercise

Look in your diary, be it a paper or electronic version such as Microsoft Outlook or Lotus Notes. If I were to invite you to a meeting at your place of work to discuss your progress on managing your time, how easy would it be to arrange for about four weeks' time?

Most people look in their diaries four weeks ahead, and apart from the odd meeting or holiday, their diary pages are virgin white. The entries that are in the diary seem to involve other people, e.g. meetings, interviews, visits.

> Cancelitis – unless the person becomes start-line focused and spreads the workload, pressures will always arise nearing deadlines, increasing the likelihood of having to cancel everything else.

To me, this implies that other people's work and needs are infinitely more important than their own. I have this vision of them rushing up and down the office, begging people to fill their diary. 'Look there is nothing in at all for the week of the 21st. I don't know how I can possibly fill my day. I have nothing to do that is important or that needs my time. So please, call me to a meeting or ask me to do something, so that I can fill these blank diary pages!'

Ridiculous? Far-fetched? Then show me in their diary where they have blocked off time for **their** work, **their** projects and **their** priorities. Unlike you, who will of course have these blocked in already, my contention is that most of your colleagues only have time booked into their diary to do with other people. Rarely do they have time booked in for personal work.

Consequently, they seem to have a blind spot for deadlines. As one approaches, they are still happily looking in their diaries, seeing blank pages and agreeing to meetings and other commitments that they can ill afford. Ill afford, that is, if they want to achieve their own objectives on time. And they can ill afford if they do not want to upset their people. For instance, look at Figure 8.

Diary management

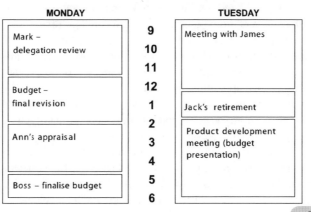

Figure 8

This is based on an example given by international time management researcher and consultant James Noon in *Start Time Forward.*

At the time the "Meeting with James" was booked, your diary was fairly empty, as we discussed above. As the four weeks becomes three weeks and then two weeks, fitting in a product development meeting, Ann's appraisal and Mark's delegation review present no problems. However, with about a week to go, when the boss wants a meeting to finalise your budget and you realise you need time to prepare for this, the diary suddenly starts to look crowded.

Your boss's throwaway remark ('You're then making a presentation to the product meeting on the impact of your final agreed budget.') really causes you problems. You have no spare slots. Even the lunchtime before the meeting is filled with the promised buffet lunch for Jack's retirement. These overcrowded schedules remind us of the famous quote:

There cannot be a crisis next week. My schedule is already full.
Henry Kissinger, Former US Secretary of State

Based on observation of the personal working practices of thousands of people in different occupational groups in different parts of the world, James Noon's work suggests that:

1. When appointments are booked some four weeks earlier, the diary page is often completely or mainly empty (as we have just discussed).
2. Gradually appointments are added in as the date approaches.
3. These appointments are based on time slots available rather than importance, and can produce the overcrowding shown in Figure 8.
4. Most people tend to agree start times, but not finish times. They fail to ask 'How long do we need?' thus losing further control of their time.
5. There is no diary booking of "personal" time for personal work.
6. Most people therefore have to achieve their own tasks in "residual time", or "the leftovers" from other people's calls on their time.
7. People can thus feel boxed in with little opportunity to respond to the "expected unexpected" work that will inevitably arrive on the day, or to prepare for their people-related appointments, or to do the follow-up work that such appointments usually bring.
8. The most common options such managers choose are to: cancel or delay; "steal" time from other important, but later, projects; cut corners on quality; or work longer hours. These are all stressful options.
9. The people most likely to suffer are the manager's direct reports over whom they have most control. So in Figure 8, it is easier to cancel or delay Mark's delegation review and Ann's appraisal than to change the boss's budget meeting or to rearrange the product meeting.
10. The solution to all these problems is to book time for yourself and to use a flexible daily plan.

"You" time

The simple ideas are often the best. The squiggle is one such idea! To prevent the sort of diary congestion we have just discussed, Noon advocates that on a four-week rolling basis, we reserve some time in our diaries for us to do our own important planned work. At this four-week "blank diary page" distance we may not know what work this will be. The solution lies in marking part of each working day with either a pencilled squiggle in our paper diary or a block of time in our electronic diary.

This blocked time acts as a reminder to us when we go into our diary that we will need some time each day for our own important work. It prevents us from over-committing ourselves and working in the "leftovers" of our time. This time for "you" may involve working with others, but should almost always involve some time working by yourself. Precisely how you can best use this "you" time may only become evident a day or so beforehand or on the day itself.

The question of how much time we should pencil in each day leads us to Noon's other proven technique.

The flexible daily framework

We will look at how we plan and prioritise our day in more detail in the next Session, but unless we plan ahead by reserving some "you" time, we will have little control, and, therefore, high levels of stress. In Session Four we will look at ways of defending this "you" time.

> Unless we plan ahead by reserving some "you" time, we will have little control, and, therefore, high levels of stress.

For now, let us consider how much time we should reserve. Any recommendations will need to take into account:

- Time for our own planned, important work.
- Time to react to other important work during the day.

Noon's response is the robust model of Figure 9. On the left is the suggested guideline for a typical day. This shows about 5 to 10% of time spent planning, probably at the beginning and end of the day. 45% is "you" time for your own important planned work. This is work that will help to achieve your own objectives and may involve working on your own or attending a meeting. Finally, most people need to allow at least 25% of their time to respond to other important matters that arise on the day. In other words, expect the unexpected and allow enough time to cope with this.

Flexible daily plan

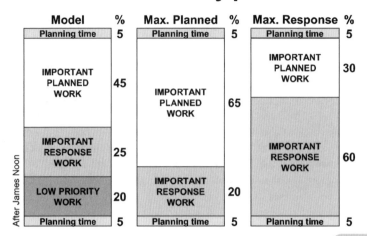

Model	%	Max. Planned	%	Max. Response	%
Planning time	5	Planning time	5	Planning time	5
IMPORTANT PLANNED WORK	45	IMPORTANT PLANNED WORK	65	IMPORTANT PLANNED WORK	30
IMPORTANT RESPONSE WORK	25			IMPORTANT RESPONSE WORK	60
LOW PRIORITY WORK	20	IMPORTANT RESPONSE WORK	20		
Planning time	5	Planning time	5	Planning time	5

After James Noon

Figure 9

When the important planned work and the planned response work is done, we can turn our attention to the lower priority tasks we all have. It is these lower priority tasks that will feel the squeeze on days when we require more time for major work of our own or when there is a crisis for which we need more response time. These lower priority tasks are often the very tasks with which we start our day in order to get some "quick ticks" on our "To Do" lists. We will discuss this more fully in the next Session.

Noon's guidance is that when we expand the time allocated to our own important work, we should always allow at least 25% of the day for the important tasks that will come along and need a same-day response. Similarly, when the crisis of the day is a big one and we have to allocate most of the day to resolve it, we should still aim to safeguard at least 30% of our time to work on our own important planned tasks. You will note that extending hours does not feature in these guidelines. The key focus is on what is important.

Of course there will always be days when the model is thrown out of the window and all our time is spent sorting out a major problem. But how many of your days are really like this? Normally there are not that many. Similarly, there are some, though probably not many days, when you do not have any crises or requests that need a same-day response. This extra time is then a bonus.

In summary, the guideline is to reserve 30-45% of your day on a rolling four-week basis. This denotes your "you" time for important planned work. This will greatly increase the likelihood of you completing your work on time and to the required standard. If it is politically unacceptable to reserve such a large percentage of your time on your electronic diary, at least block some "you" time for when you want to work by yourself. Related meetings can be shown separately.

6. Schedules and timeframes – get real!

Handling scheduling conflicts

The verb "to schedule" is defined as to arrange or plan an event to occur at a particular time. Techniques for scheduling ahead that we have covered so far are: the "you" time squiggle, start-line-focused projects, and action planning with interim milestones. From Noon's research, we now cover three further techniques: sensitive time, the two deadlines per week rule, and bringing work forward.

If ever we need to expect the unexpected, it is surely around the time of a major deadline. There is usually last-minute work to complete and queries to solve immediately before, and sometimes just after, the due date. Noon calls this "sensitive time", and finds it usually falls over a one to five-day period, depending on the complexity of the task and the quality of our earlier project control.

Given this two to three-day average sensitive time, it seems prudent to limit our project deadlines to a maximum of two per week as a guideline. Where there is a potential clash, seek opportunities to pull some work forward and complete it earlier.

For instance, if you were responsible for managing a sales conference, overseeing a product launch at it, making one of the conference presentations, and producing a company video to show there, you are surely courting disaster. However, plan to finish the video a couple of weeks earlier and have the product launch wrapped up the week before, and you can concentrate on your presentation and last-minute conference administration with a lighter heart.

This will not happen by itself though. If you are participating in numerous projects, draw lines on a chart to show start and finish times and any interim milestones. You can then spot potential conflicts and reschedule accordingly. As with all scheduling, do it early.

Estimating time frames

'Under-promise and over-deliver' is a good maxim for excellent customer service. Too many people do the opposite – they over-promise and under-deliver. They promise Wednesday but it takes till Friday. They consistently underestimate how long a task will take. They gain a reputation for being unrealistic with their timescales.

Many such people wear rose-tinted glasses. They only see the ideal scenario. They estimate a task will take three days to complete, so they promise three days. So often this means three days to complete provided they have nothing else to do, suffer no interruptions, and receive no other calls on their time. Of course, in most cases, this is quite unrealistic.

Here are four simple tips for any such colleagues you may have.

1. The "Get Real" Question

Whenever they promise a date, ask them if it is realistic. What other tasks have they currently got on? Have they allowed time to deal with any emergencies that may occur, or do they rely on Henry Kissinger's famous quote mentioned earlier? Remind such people that it is better to quote a later date and achieve it than quote an earlier date and miss it.

2. The Mini-Max Technique

This consists of setting two separate markers – the best scenario and the worst scenario. If everything goes like clockwork, there are no hold-ups or distractions, and everyone involved in the project is immediately available when needed, what is the best time that can be achieved – the best scenario?

On the other hand, if there are delays with other people being on holiday, or suppliers being late, emergencies occur and mayhem breaks out, what is the longest time this might take – the worst scenario?

You do not necessarily then just split the difference. Rather, you apply your judgement and knowledge of the situation to decide which of the two scenarios is the more likely. For instance, if a brochure could be produced between a best scenario of five days and worst scenario of twenty days, you might decide on, say, eight days if you knew the job was straightforward and the printer was quiet. On the other hand, you might set something nearer the twenty days if the people needed to sign off the proofs are rarely in the office and the printer is in a very busy period.

3. The Double-It Technique

Think of a number and double it – it hardly sounds like a technique. But its basis is the planned reactive time of the typical day – 25% up to as much as 60%. On that basis, if you believe a task will take two days to complete, many people will need to add another one to two days for likely interruptions, making three or four days to do the job, not two. So take the idea and adapt it. Expect the unexpected and build in time accordingly.

4. The Communications Factor

If you are reliant on someone else completing a key step by a certain date, make sure you let them know and that they agree they can do it. As the old saying goes, when we ASS/U/ME we make an ass out of u and me. Communicate your plan and get acceptance as well as understanding.

Action Plan Case Study

Now that we have covered setting objectives, action planning, scheduling and estimating, it is time for hands-on experience. First try the following case study, then two of your own. The case study situation is:

> Chris Taylor and her business partner Brian Powell want to upgrade the computer for their small business. It is now early April and they have fixed a meeting for the 28th April to decide what hardware and software they need. In the meantime they will both look through computer magazines to see what is available.
>
> Brian is then attending a computer fair on the 9th May whilst Chris is on holiday. They will make their final decision on the 28th May, just before Brian goes on holiday (the day after). They will place their order on the 1st June to get maximum credit and want the new machine installed before the 14th July. On that date, Sue Pear, a new trainee, will join them. A week's training given by the provider is wanted for the week commencing the 4th August, by which time Sue will have completed her induction programme. Chris, Brian and Sue will then need to practise using the new equipment and software before the 13th September. On that date they have advertising booked for a direct mail pilot campaign, whilst the main campaign is scheduled to start on the 8th October.
>
> To help ensure everything goes to plan, Chris and Brian have asked you to draw up an action plan to summarise all this. To save you time, they have listed the key milestones, albeit in alphabetical order. Rearrange these in the correct sequence, allocating dates and initials for accountability. You can compare your plan with the one suggested at the end of this Session.
>
> **Objective:** To upgrade our computer to an agreed specification and budget and enable us to carry out our direct mail campaign starting the 8th October.

Accountable: CT/BP   Start date: 1st April   End date: 8th October

Action step (WHAT)	Action step (WHAT)	WHO?	WHEN?
Agree needs			
Assess market – fair			
Assess market – magazines			
Decide on provider			
Installation			
Investigate providers			
Place order			
Practise			
Shortlist providers			
Start full programme			
Start pilot programme			
Training			

Your Action Plans

Battles are won on the drawing board, then on the field. Napoleon

On pages 25-26, you were asked to write worthwhile business and personal objectives. To help ensure you achieve these, use the format you have just tried in the case study, and write out an action plan for each objective using the templates on the next page.

When you have completed one or both, talk them through with a friend or colleague. A single page summary will be a very helpful format to facilitate discussion. It will allow you to: assess the realism of the schedule; share responsibility for action; spot if anything has been missed out; and gain agreement to go forward.

Business objective title from page 25:

ACTION STEP (WHAT is to be done)	WHO will do this?	By WHEN to complete?

Personal objective title from page 26:		
ACTION STEP (WHAT is to be done)	WHO will do this?	By WHEN to complete?

7. Monitoring – goodbye to control freaks and metal coffins!

Having established our objective and action plan of who will do what by when to make it happen, how do we make sure that it will happen? The answer lies in effective controls. They come in a four-part set. You need all four. Miss out any one and you could be in trouble.

1. Set standards

What exactly do you want to achieve? How will you know when you have achieved it? SMARTER objectives will spell this out.

2. Measure performance

What and how will you measure? Some measurements are easier than others. It is usually easy to measure sales or production, but less easy to measure customer service or product quality. Whilst all these factors **can** be measured, you need to decide what you **will** measure and how you will do it.

3. Evaluate performance

Evaluate the quality and quantity of the information obtained from measuring performance, and establish whether you are in front of, or behind, where you want to be.

4. Take corrective action

If you were driving on the wrong side of the road, with a large vehicle coming t owards you, you would not be content to say, 'If I carry on like this we are going to crash', you would take evasive action! Similarly, in controlling performance, if you are not happy with progress, take corrective action. In other words, do not just sit there – do something!

Planning without controlling is a complete waste of time. Your job is to make things happen, not just hope they will happen. But whilst control is important, you should not go over the top.

Over-zealous control freaks have given controlling a bad press recently. In this age of empowering people, they have been rightly frowned upon for crowding their people with overly tight and prescriptive controls. I am all in favour of the 3As approach:

> **Agree** what you want them to do.
> **Assist** them when they need and ask for your help. But then…
> **Allow** them to get on with it!

So, if you have any control freak friends, urge them to have the operation. Have the anorak surgically removed and, with it, the worst excesses of oppressive and stifling controls. We want effective controls that are simple and visual. Visual? Yes, visual. Beware of the metal coffin! Too many well-constructed plans and controls are buried in metal coffins – also known as filing cabinets. They rarely see the light of day again. Visual controls are always in sight and, therefore, in mind. This simple and visual combination can be found in our earlier friend, the action plan.

On a single page in an organiser or on a PC screen, you can not only spell out your SMARTER objective, but the milestones of who will do what by when to achieve it. The "by when" column provides the simple visual control. Set pre-arranged review dates and you have an effective combination of freedom and control.

These simple action plans will enable us to link our medium-term plans and projects into our daily plans. We will look at this in the next Session.

8. Personal planning – is there life after work?

If you listed your aims in the importance exercise in Session One, odds are that you do have or want to have a life outside work. I hope so. It has long been recognised that all work and no play make Jack a dull boy. Dull boys and girls have less to offer their organisation than their more rounded colleagues who have heeded the advice to "get a life!"

The point to be made here is that all of these techniques can be used at home as well as at work. Some people – some families – have gone so far as to agree a family mission statement based on their shared values and vision of the family life they all want. Others find this more attuned to an American culture than a British one and do not get involved.

However, even if you feel that some of the ideas are fine for work but not for home, please do not dismiss them out of hand. Rather, pick out those that you might find useful for domestic purposes and use them. Deciding what is important, setting goals, and using action plans, can be just as helpful to the working parent juggling a career, house, family and hobbies, as it can to the executive trying to cram more into the working day.

So the recommendation is to use some of these ideas in the home as well as the office, without becoming the time management bore of the millennium.

Suggested Answers To Session Exercises

Spot The Smart Objective

There is no single right answer to these, as we know nothing about the company context in which they are set. However, the point of the exercise was to get you analysing objectives. So here are a few thoughts:

1. **To increase sales by 10%.**

   - This might be fine as a high-level company goal, but it is certainly not a SMART objective.
   - There is no timescale and no indication of whether it is for all or some market sectors, sales teams or individuals.

2. **To launch Product X by the end of the second quarter.**

   - Again, as a high-level corporate or divisional aim it might be fine.
   - But unless it is made a lot SMARTER, there could be considerable dispute after the launch as to whether it was a success.
   - Adding suitable **success criteria** can transform it, for instance:
     - Pricing, sales and promotional policies are agreed by the January board meeting.
     - The launch creates first year sales of £1.5 million, at a minimum gross margin of 26%.
     - We achieve a distribution of at least 200 dealerships.

3. **To improve the credit position from 82 days to 60 days by the end of the financial year and maintain it at or below that level thereafter.**

    - We have a time frame and a measurable "days" credit figure.
    - In most companies it would be specific enough, as there is usually only one overall "days" credit figure quoted. If there were more than one, further clarification may be needed.
    - Is it realistic? We cannot tell from the information we have. If it is at the start of the financial year it might be. But if there are only a couple of months to go it probably is not.
    - To motivate the team to achieve it, it will need to be agreed by them as being achievable.

4. **To improve the performance of the retail sales force by:**

    - Increasing their calls per day.
    - Reducing their miles per call.
    - Better prospecting.

    - Again, as a general intent, it gives a direction, but is far from being SMART.
    - If we increase sales from an average of 80 calls per month to 81 is that acceptable? Or should we spell out the sort of percentage improvement in calls and miles we are looking for?
    - What is "better prospecting"? Whether we mean quantity of prospecting, quality of calls, or something else is not stated. To make the prospecting bit SMART, we need to say something like:
        - To improve prospecting by reducing the quotations-to-order ratio from 1.7 to 1.5, and the number of prospect calls per new account from 5.7 to 4.
    - This implies that we know, or can find out, what they currently are. If we cannot, then we have no yardstick to measure against and need to suggest something else.

5. **To identify a suitable venue for the 2006 spring exhibition which:**

    - Has good road and rail links.
    - Projects a professional image.
    - Will keep within budget.
    - Has a suitable room.
    - Is available for three days in the second week of March.
    - As it stands, measuring the successful achievement of this could be very subjective. Good links, a professional image, and a suitable room, might all be interpreted differently by different people.
    - However, by adding further criteria, such as 'has the prior approval of the sales team', this subjectivity can be considerably reduced and the objective thereby made much SMARTER.

The Action Plan Case Study – Suggested Answer

Action step (WHAT)	Action step (WHAT)	WHO?	WHEN?
Agree needs	Assess market – magazines	CT/BP	Apr/May
Assess market – fair	Agree needs	CT/BP	28 Apr
Assess market – magazines	Assess market – fair	BP	9 May
Decide on provider	Shortlist providers	BP	May
Installation	Investigate providers	BP	May
Investigate providers	Decide on provider	CT/BP	28 May
Place order	Place order	CT	1 June
Practise	Installation	Provider	By 14 July
Shortlist providers	Training	Provider	4-8 Aug
Start full programme	Practise	All	Aug/Sep
Start pilot programme	Start pilot programme	All	13 Sep
Training	Start full programme	All	8 Oct

Normally, to avoid confusion, it is best to have just one person accountable for each stage. However, as the case study was of a small company with joint owners, both names have been put down for some key decisions.

SUMMARY OF SESSION TWO: Planning Ahead

1. To plan and prioritise effectively, you need clarity about your role and what is expected of you.
2. Determine the Key Result Areas of your job and look for opportunities to improve each one.
3. Agree SMARTER objectives to reach a consensus about exactly what you are trying to achieve.
4. Start-line-focused Action Plans spread the workload, improve work quality, reduce stress and provide a simple way of monitoring results.
5. Plan time in your diary for your personal projects and objectives as well as those of other people, using the "you" time squiggle or electronic diary blocking techniques.
6. Schedule a maximum of two major deadlines per week, bringing work forward to avoid conflicts if necessary. Set realistic time scales which allow for "real world" situations.
7. Planning without controlling is a waste of time. But keep controls simple, appropriate for the person and the task, and visible – in sight and in mind.
8. Good time management ideas can be used at home as well as work.

Session

3

Session Three: Planning And Prioritising The Day

Assuming you do not suffer from the Chicken Farmer Syndrome explained in Session One, this Session looks at how you currently plan your day and asks – "Is there a better way?" We cover:

1. The best way to plan the day.
2. Advanced prioritising.
3. How to link medium-term plans with daily plans.
4. Daily scheduling considerations.
5. Committed time – what it is and how to use it.
6. Some practicalities to turn theory into practice.
7. And finally… more general hints on getting the best from each day.

1. The best way to plan the day

So how do you plan your day? And what has the following century-old true story got to do with whether you could plan it better?

> As you will recall, Charles M. Schwab (1862-1939) grew from unskilled labourer to President of Bethlehem Steel, the world's largest independent steel producer. By the 1920s, he was one of the first people to earn a million-dollar salary. Always keen to improve the productivity of himself and his people, Schwab engaged the services of Ivy L. Lee, a well-known management consultant of the day. 'Show me a way to get more things done with my time and I'll pay any fee within reason,' said Schwab. Lee, however, refused to invoice for his advice, commenting, 'Only pay me if it works and send me a cheque for what you think it's worth.'

> Shortly afterwards, Lee received a cheque for $25,000, estimated to be more than ten times that in today's money. Asked how he could justify such an enormous payment, Schwab described the idea as the most profitable piece of business advice he had ever received.

And it is yours now, not for $250,000 or even $25,000, but just for the price of this book! This story and daily planning method continue to dominate today's time management books and articles. Twenty-first century research shows the method still works, helped by some refinements introduced over the last thirty years. We will examine the method in outline in Figure 10 and then discuss the detail.

1. Write a daily "To Do" list
Note the word is **"daily"** not "some days" or even "most days". Time management guru Alan Lakein shares this view. Over the years, he found that highly effective people made daily "To Do" lists, whilst less effective people often knew about them but only wrote them sporadically. Conclusion: only a daily "To Do" will do! Even the minority that can manage on a weekly list need to look at it daily and update it as needed.

This advice also ties in with the subconscious brain research mentioned in the previous Session. When we have more than about seven things to remember we struggle. Some items get pushed to the back of the mind and are easily forgotten. Thus the antidote to forgetting things is to write them down in one place on your daily "To Do" list, be it paper or electronic.

Daily planning summary

1. Write a daily "To Do" list.

2. Prioritise by importance.

3. Start on the most important task first.

4. Complete one task before starting another.

5. Work through in order of importance.

6. Don't worry if you don't complete everything.

Figure 10

This raises the question of how many items should we include in our list. There are two extremes. Ivy Lee advised only writing down the five or six most important tasks. Whilst this will help you to focus on doing the right things, it does not help you to remember the other smaller tasks that you want to complete. On the other hand, I have seen people with huge lists, which they have no chance of tackling. This can be depressing for them and any people who work with them, as promises and commitments are often not met.

I therefore recommend and operate a middle course. This ensures that my daily "To Do" list includes everything I would like to do in the day, without overwhelming me. Of particular value here is the monthly "To Do" list, which we will discuss in section 3.

2. Prioritise by importance
There are two methods we shall cover. One is the simple 1-2-3 approach where 1 is the most important, 2 the next most important and so on. The second is more sophisticated and is based on an important-urgent matrix. Both systems are more helpful and specific than some of the computer software options that offer High-Medium-Low priorities. Whilst it is true that all highly important tasks are equally highly important, it does not help you decide, on a pragmatic daily basis, which one to do first. This may be wonderful for the career procrastinator, who can think about it but do nothing. However, the rest of us need to get started!

3. Start on the most important task first

Which do your colleagues currently start with? The quickest? The easiest? The ones that will get some ticks on their list? Or the hardest – to get it out of the way? Or the task that was given last or loudest perhaps? Or anything but the task they do not want to do and keep putting off? I have every confidence that you are not guilty of any of these, so here are a few tips to pass on to your more errant friends:

- The trouble with the "quickest and easiest tasks first" routine is that you can end the day with lots of ticks that look good. However, the ones that are missing are probably the important, challenging and value-adding items such as the strategic three-year review or that improvement proposal you keep meaning to do. In addition, these quick and easy tasks are probably the "low priority work" we saw in Figure 9 of the last Session. These are exactly the tasks which should get squeezed out if we need to maximise either our planned or response important work.
- Hardest first is better in that it helps to get over some procrastination. This is fine, so long as the hardest also happens to be the most important. But I suspect they will not always match.
- Prioritising based on the job you were just given or just picked up puts you back in our first Session's Chicken Farmer territory.
- And responding to "whoever shouts loudest" has someone else in control of your time and your life, not you.
- So the best option, one that will consistently deliver high performance and personal satisfaction, is the one that bases your priorities on importance.

4. Complete one task before starting another

Have you ever sat at your desk, part-way through a project, when – panic! You remember another task you need to do. So you stop what you are doing on the project. You begin this other job and off you go, only to have a guilt attack part-way through because you have not done anything about project X. So, yet again, you stop and start something else. Stop and start. Stop and start. Lots started. Little finished. Lots of effort. Little to show for it. Lots of good intentions.

> The best option, one that will consistently deliver high performance and personal satisfaction, is the one that bases your priorities on importance.

Little real job satisfaction, and possibly a great deal of stress.

The answer is to finish one task before you start another. But what about big projects I hear you cry? They may take months. We cannot ignore everything else until we have finished the project. You are, as ever, quite right. The answer here is to split the project into bite-sized, digestible tasks. Finish one of these mini-tasks before moving on to something else.

5. Work through in order of importance

So after the most important, start on the second most important and so on. What could be simpler? In theory nothing. It's not rocket science and it's not difficult. But if it is different to your current method, it will take time and effort to get used to. The rewards of improved performance and satisfaction are well worth the effort though. Prove it to yourself.

6. Don't worry if you don't complete everything

Ivy Lee's advice here was that even if you don't finish everything on your list, you would at least have been working on what was important, before reaching the less important. He also asserted that if you cannot achieve your work this way, you cannot do it any other way either. Remaining tasks can be transferred to the next day's "To Do" list.

A hundred years on and there is still widespread support for Lee's basic approach. However, we can add some refinements developed and adapted from the work of more modern writers such as Claus Möeller, John Adair, Stephen Covey and James Noon. These include advanced prioritising (section 2) and the use of a monthly as well as a daily "To Do" list (section 3).

2. Advanced prioritising

Urgent-important matrix

	URGENT	NOT URGENT
IMPORTANT	**A** Important and urgent	**B** Important but not urgent
NOT IMPORTANT	**C** Urgent but not important	**D** Not urgent and not important

Figure 11

The simple prioritising method mentioned earlier is fine if you only have a few tasks. For more complex days, you need further help. The following method is tried, tested and recommended. It is based on the matrix shown in Figure 11. It raises the question, 'Do you spend too much time boxed into the wrong box?' Let me first explain each box in turn.

A's are for ACTIONING

These tasks are both urgent and important, and therefore need to be actioned now. Virtually all of us have some "A" important and urgent tasks to do each day. This only becomes a problem if the urgency part becomes an addiction, causing "busy sickness". Symptoms include rushing around in a highly visible, frantic, reactive Mr or Ms Fixit mode and getting high on adrenalin.   Causes are often an underlying crisis management culture (which will be discussed more fully in Session Five). Suffice it to say here that too much time in the "A" box might lead to stress, but will certainly keep people out of the all-important "B" box.

B's are for BUILDING

These tasks are important, though not urgent. They are the tasks that will build and add real value to your own personal development and that of your organisation. Yet how often have you had the important squeezed out by the urgent? Here are some examples of B's which most course participants can relate to:

- **Meetings** – ensuring adequate preparation and follow-up time.
- **Delegation** – thinking through what is needed and making time to review progress.
- **Personal projects** – doing them as opposed to meaning to do them some day.
- **Policies and procedures** – improving them rather than tolerating their imperfections.
- **Teams** – being available to motivate, coach and lead your people.
- **Relationships** – spending more time with internal and external customers, family and friends.
- **Direction** – setting clear objectives and action plans to achieve them both professionally and privately.
- **Personal development** – making time to think, be creative, and maintain your continuing professional development.

We will come to your own examples of B's shortly.

C's are for CURTAILING

These tasks are urgent but not important. Time in this box needs curtailing because, for most people, it is more like a black hole into which their time disappears. Warning signs are when you hear comments such as, 'I'll just clear these emails first', or 'It won't take a minute just to knock these little jobs off before I do anything else'. Beware! Research quoted by the Covey organisation suggests that most of us spend over half our day doing work that is urgent but not important – the low priority work mentioned in the previous chapter. By contrast, highly effective people spend over half their day in the "B" box (see Figure 12).

Prioritising matrix

A **Urgent/Important** Major tasks: do well Average: 20-30% HEO: 20%	B **Important/Not urgent** Value-adding tasks Average: 15% HEO: 65%
C **Urgent/Not important** Minor tasks: fit round eggs Average: 50-60% HEO: 15%	D **Not urgent/Not important** Do these tasks need doing? Average: 2-3% HEO: less than 1%

HEO = Highly Effective Organisations (Adapted from Covey Leadership Center Inc.)

Figure 12

The quickest way for most people to make an immediate improvement in their performance is to control and drastically curtail the time they spend in the urgent but not important "C" box, and spend much more time in the important but not urgent "B" box.

D's are for DITCHING

Being neither important nor urgent, we should spend virtually no time in this box. At home, Internet usage, video games and watching TV might sometimes belong here for some people. Whilst most of us integrate these activities into our lives in a balanced, healthy way, for some they are the new addictions. At work, activities here include junk mail and junk email and other time wasting activities.

I agree with James Noon's comments that 'we cannot go on and on doing more work in shorter time just because the work is there to be done.' He advocates a "reductionist" approach, focusing only on what is important, and leaving unimportant work not done. Eliminating "D" tasks and drastically curtailing time spent on "C" tasks are necessary steps in this direction. A further useful step is for you to list some of your own "B" tasks…

Exercise "B"

Using the "B" examples used earlier as a guide, write down examples of your own important but not urgent tasks.

Business and professional examples:

Personal development examples:

The quickest way for most people to make an immediate improvement in their performance is to control and drastically curtail the time they spend in the urgent but not important "C" box, and spend much more time in the important but not urgent "B" box.

Summary

Having fine-tuned Ivy Lee's need to prioritise with this important/urgent matrix, we can now fine-tune his "To Do" list...

3. How to link medium-term plans with daily plans

Have you ever written something important on a "To Do" list, not done it, and so rewritten it on the next list, and the next, and the next? So have I. What a drag! Although Ivy Lee recommended carrying uncompleted tasks to the next day, it is the kind of behaviour that gives "To Do" lists a bad name. There is a remedy.

It is called the Monthly Objectives List or the "B" Task List. On this list, be it paper or on screen, you record all the important tasks to be achieved in the month, over and above the daily routines. Beside each one you put a target completion date. Include on this page all the milestones from the action plans discussed in Session Two that are for completion that month.

Then each day, as you make out your "To Do" list, look at your Monthly Objectives List and transfer across any task that needs action today if you are to meet your deadline. This "B" thereupon becomes one of your "A's". It is now urgent as well as important. Provided your monthly list is always in sight, and therefore, in mind, it will act as a constant reminder to include your important medium-term plans amongst the day's other urgent and pressing matters.

You might trial a page pinned in front of you at your workstation, a separate screen on your laptop, or a page in your organiser. My personal preference is for a monthly objectives overview page in my paper organiser, which is specially designed to fold into each daily plan. It constantly haunts me, refusing to go away, and acts as a permanent reminder to include the important along with the urgent. It also acts as a control mechanism to show me how many of my monthly objectives I have achieved and which are outstanding. I have an ongoing love-hate relationship with it!

Prioritising summary

My daily "To Do" list only has A's and C's, numbered A1, A2, A3 and C1, C2, C3, etc. D's – the not important and not urgent tasks, which seemed like a good idea at the time, rarely get a look in. They usually fall off the page – not done and not missed. Feel free to do likewise and sleep soundly! Donate time saved on D's to work on the all-important B's.

As an antidote to procrastination on A and B activities, I like the traditional quote:

> **Never put off till tomorrow what you can do today.** Anon

But for C and D activities I prefer Mark Twain:

> **Never put off till tomorrow what you can do the
> day after tomorrow just as well.**

Monthly Objectives Exercise 1

Decide where you are going to keep your monthly objectives:

Paper organiser page ❑ PC or laptop screen ❑ Pinned-up page at your desk ❑
Personal electronic organiser ❑ Other option ❑

Monthly Objectives Exercise 2

Draw up a template for your objectives with the following suggested headings:

Objectives for month of..........................	Target Date	Actual Date	✓

- One page per month helps to keep your list succinct and focused on the important.
- It should not take you more than half an hour a month to pull together all your action plan milestones and events with attendant deadlines in your calendar or diary.
- Make sure your list remains "in sight and in mind".

Monthly Objectives Exercise 3

Once you have set up your template, why not complete it for this month (or next month if appropriate)? There is no time like the present, or as Francis Quarles has it:

One today is worth two tomorrows.

4. Daily scheduling considerations

The all-year breakfast

Here is a memorable dish to help you plan, prioritise and schedule each day.

You will need 300 grams of dry rice (any type), three medium-sized eggs, three eggcups, a container for the rice, and an empty pint or half-litre transparent beer glass.

Put all the rice in the beer glass and put the eggs on top. You will find that they don't fit! The eggs will stick up over the rim of the glass. This is to remind you that many workdays are like this. You seem to have more work to do than will fit into the time available. And with the sheer amount of detailed tasks facing you, like all those grains of rice, there is simply no room for the big, important B jobs, like the three eggs.

Now put the eggs in the eggcups and tip the rice back into its container.

This time, think about Ivy Lee and his approach. Start with the most important, work through it until you have finished, then start with the next most important etc. Apply this to the all-year breakfast!

Put the three eggs in the beer glass first. Now add the rice. You can get most of the rice in as it fits around the eggs. Look closely. You will see some gaps around the eggs. Shake the glass and fill these gaps with the rice. Now even more of the rice **and** the eggs will fit in the glass, though not **all** the rice.

Just as you have gaps around your eggs, you have gaps in your day. For example, a meeting finishes early, someone is late for an appointment, and you have five minutes before lunch. You can use these gaps to knock off some quick jobs – some of your C's. Make some quick phone calls, send an email, do some filing, read that article. However, even then you will have some jobs left over unfinished. Provided you have followed the method, at least you know that you have been working on what's important. In these circumstances, I echo Ivy Lee's advice to Charles Schwab – don't worry if you don't finish everything on your list.

So the recipe for the all-year breakfast is to deal with your eggs first, fit the rest of the day around them, and you've cracked it! By the way, did I mention the eggs should be hard-boiled?

Don't over-plan

How practical is it to plan every minute of the day from the moment you walk into work to the moment you leave?

Correct! It's not at all practical. Few people would last more than ten minutes before the phone would ring, or the boss would come in, or the system would go down or something similar would occur to throw your plan out the window! So when scheduling the day, plan any fixed items, such as any form of meeting and the "A" time you have blocked in your diary that we spoke of in the last section.

Use Noon's model in Figure 9 (which we covered in Session 2) to give you a mental picture of the shape of the day. Stay focused on the planned and unplanned important "eggs", and fit in the less important "rice" around these as time allows.

Re-prioritise as needed

We have spoken of the need to be flexible in order to cope with what the day throws at us. And here, the human soul is infinitely better equipped than the rest of the animal kingdom.

From your school days you will remember the Stimulus → Response cycle in animals. If the stimulus is threatening in any way, it triggers a flow of adrenaline resulting in either a "fight" or "flight" response. Unfortunately, some of your colleagues still react this way to certain events that threaten to disrupt their daily plans and priorities! Some give a knee-jerk reaction and either fight the intrusion and maybe lose a few friends, or roll over, accept the intrusion, and put it at the top of their priorities.

Just explain to them that we humans can have an intervening "Think" process between the "Stimulus" and "Response". We can consider each new demand on our time, be it an email, a telephone call, a colleague needing help, something wanted by the boss, or whatever, in the light of our objectives and existing priorities.

For instance, just because the boss asks you for something, it does not necessarily mean that it is wanted immediately. By simply asking, 'When do you need this by?', you can determine if you really do need to drop everything and start on it right away, or whether it can wait until you have finished what you are doing, or even wait until next Tuesday.

Similarly with colleagues, if you can find out when they need it and why, it will help you decide whether you can or cannot meet their expectations in the light of all the other things you have to do.

> Stimulus → Response: the choice of Chicken Farmers.
> Stimulus → Think → Response: the right priority choice for you!

Quality time for quality tasks

Are you a lark or an owl? In other words, are you at your best early in the day or later on? We all have slightly different body clocks and energy levels. A lark can be bright and breezy at breakfast but start to fade later in the day. On the other hand, some owls look like zombies at breakfast and find it hard to have civil conversations before mid-morning, but when the larks start to fade, these owls come into their own!

The energy curve

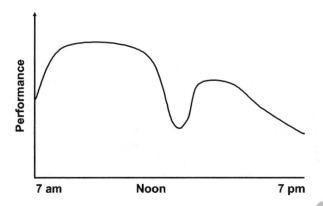

Figure 13

So, bearing that in mind, look at the energy curve in Figure 13. How similar or dissimilar are you? The point is that the time to tackle your important tasks is when you are feeling at your best. Do the other, less important, more routine jobs, at other times of the day.

If you can choose, try having meetings or discussions with people outside your "peak energy" time. Hopefully you will be stimulated by the interaction and kept interested, keeping your quality time for your quality tasks (if your meetings are not stimulating, look for ideas to change them in Session Five).

Beware of extended hours

Many people tackle heavy workloads by coming in early and/or staying late. 'I usually get more done in that first hour or after hours,' they say, 'than I do in the rest of the day.' Oh yes? Well before you let them get away with that sort of statement, get them to consider the following points:

1. Even as you read this, sales trainers up and down the land are advising their charges to try telephoning outside of normal working hours in order to get round any "castle guards" or call-screening systems surrounding their prey, sorry, prospects. They may be the only person in and may answer the phone themselves. If so, it can disrupt their "uninterrupted time".

2. Even if they are not prone to receiving disruptive outside calls, what about their own colleagues? They can also get to know about these longer hours. If colleagues find it difficult to trap them, sorry, track them down in the day, they too sometimes decide either to phone or to call round personally in the knowledge they will see them, albeit by disturbing their "undisturbed" time.

3. And what about the energy curve we were just discussing? For most people, the early and late additional hours do not coincide with the best time on their energy curve. They may, therefore, be trying to work on important tasks when they are not feeling at their best. This often affects either the quality of their work or the length of time it takes them to do it.

4. Then there is Parkinson's Law, with its "work expanding to fill the time available". If managers get into a routine of coming in at 7am and working until 7pm, then the work tends to take that long.

5. If managers feel they can only do important work at the beginning and end of the day, what are they doing in between? There is a danger they maybe take longer over meetings, writing reports etc., are keener on the "my door is always open" policy, and make themselves more available than most. This can create an impression of being more relaxed and having more time than others. In turn, this can result in their being given more work! This means they have to work longer hours, which means that…

For most people then, working longer hours is not the best answer to their time management problems. **Making better use of their working day is**. We will be looking at this again in Session Four.

5. Committed time – what it is and how to use it

By "committed time" I mean time you have committed for a particular task or activity. This can be anything from attending a meeting, going to the doctor's, travelling to work, or doing household chores. Apparently the time is spoken for. You cannot do anything else with it. Wrong!

> The time to tackle your important tasks is when you are feeling at your best. Do the other, less important, more routine jobs, at other times of the day.

Remember the eggs and rice? Remember how there were gaps around the eggs in which you could put more rice? This is how it is with much of our committed time. It is rare nowadays for people to attend a public training course without getting on their mobile phones at breaks or lunch time to speak to the office or home, or a customer or supplier. That is making use of committed time.

We all have lots of pockets of time into which we can squeeze those little jobs which would otherwise mount up and become a major problem. Here are some specific examples:

Waiting in reception
Can you find out more about the company from the receptionist whilst you wait for your meeting, or read the company literature or catch up on trade magazines?

Meetings
If they are late starting, can you get an update from colleagues on what is happening in the rest of the organisation? Can you build bridges, strengthen relationships? Can you possibly make a phone call (so long as that will not delay the start of the meeting any further)? If the meeting finishes early, can you use the time to check your emails and send some replies?

Travel by car
This is good thinking time. Mull over some issues in your mind and/or keep up-to-date with the news. Also, do not feel guilty about relaxing to your favourite music. Sometimes, if you have had a hectic day, this might be just what you need most. Provided they are used safely within a country's legal guidelines, hands-free phones in cars have made life much more productive for many field-based people. They are an excellent way of using time committed to travel for maintaining and improving communications with colleagues and customers alike.

Travel by rail
It is quite surprising how much reading or writing you can do, even on a one or two-hour train journey. Apart from the growing trend of some overly intrusive mobile phone conversations from fellow travellers, rail journeys can be a productive time bonus rather than an unproductive bore.

Travel by plane
From short internal flights to long-haul overseas trips, committed travelling time offers a full range of opportunities for reading, writing, thinking, relaxing or catching-up on sleep. Within aircraft safety constraints, I know of some people who love, and others who loathe, the use of laptop computers on flights. Do whatever works and feels right for you.

Visits to the hairdresser, dentist etc.
Personally, I always take my own reading material to these places. If I have to wait, I would rather read my own choice of material than that of someone else!

Household chores
Some people do their ironing in front of their favourite TV programme, or listen to the test match commentary on their headphones whilst they mow the lawn. These are just some examples of using committed time to achieve more than was originally planned. The only requirement is that you are on the lookout for opportunities and prepare for them accordingly.

If a window of opportunity appears, don't pull down the shades. Tom Peters

6. Some practicalities to turn theory into practice

For starters

Ivy Lee would have us start with the most important task first. But suppose you arrive at the office at 8.50 and have a 9.00 meeting. Will you start with the most important task in this situation? Of course not. Ten minutes will not allow you enough worthwhile time. You can do some of your other, less important but quicker tasks in the ten minutes you have at your disposal.

When do you plan the day?

Ideally, it is better to plan tomorrow at the end of today because:

- You can quickly review today and see what is outstanding at the end of it.
- You are clear in your mind about what you are doing tomorrow.
- You engage the power of the subconscious mind, which can be thinking about what lies ahead. While we sleep or relax, it often makes links with past experiences, which can result in some of those seemingly spontaneous ideas and insights. So, ideally, plan the night before.

However, those of us who are larks are not always at our brightest and best at the end of the day. If the situation and job allow, we larks may prefer to plan at the start of the day. We are quicker and sharper then and it may suit us better. This can work well apart from when travel is involved. If this is the case, we clearly have no option but to plan the night before.

Personal planning and the "Oh no!" syndrome

You see sufferers all the time. You have probably been afflicted yourself. Outbreaks are sudden and stressful. Victims suddenly stop what they are doing and say things like, 'Oh no! I should have...' or 'Oh no! I meant to...' or 'Oh no! I was supposed to...'

The cause is more often than not some personal or domestic chore they agreed or meant to do but had forgotten. And why have they forgotten to do the job? Usually it is because they have not written it down. Or, if they have written it down, it is on a Post-It or scrap of paper that is easily lost.

I recommend that these simple personal tasks be added to your daily "To Do" list. Have one place for everything. Write it down and forget about it. Because you know where you wrote it, you know where to find it. And with it being under your nose all day long, you are in grave danger of being reminded to do it!

7. And finally... more general hints for each day

Efficient versus Effective

How do you define the difference between these two adjectives?   One dictionary definition can be summarised as:

> **Efficient: producing something with the least waste of effort.**
> **Effective: producing a result.**

You may prefer the abridged version:

> **Efficient: Doing things right.**
> **Effective: Doing the right things.**

Good managers of their time need to be both efficient **and** effective. They need to be efficient in the way they handle their mail, email, telephone and general administration (we discuss ways of doing this in Session Six). But they also need to be effective by focusing on those aspects of their work that will give them the best return on their time. This leads us on to:

The Pareto Principle

Vilfredo Pareto was the Italian economist who identified that 80% of a country's wealth was owned by 20% of the people. His 80/20 principle lives on today. Look at yourself for instance. You probably wear 20% of your wardrobe 80% of the time. You probably play 20% of your CDs 80% of the time.

And in many organisations, 80% of the business comes from 20% of the customers. 80% of the problems come from 20% of the products, and so on. Okay, it might not be exactly 80/20. It might be 70/30 or 90/10, but Pareto's Principle still holds good in so many aspects of our lives, including our time management.

So often, 80% of our important output comes from 20% of our time. Research shows that we can substantially boost our productivity if we:

- Identify the "vital few" tasks which produce our biggest value-adding outputs (our "eggs").
- Match our best high-energy time to these high pay-off items (quality time for quality tasks).
- Block this time in our dairy ("You" time).
- Jealously safeguard this prime time by minimising interruptions (see Session Four).

Just before we move to the next Session, let us make sure we have grasped the gist of this one…

Recap Exercise

Take five minutes or so to fill in the gaps below. The answers can be found just before the Session summary (no peeking!).

The best way to plan and prioritise our day is to start by making a (1) _____ list. We then (2) _____ employing an urgent-important matrix. Urgent and important items are classed as (3) ___'s. Urgent but not important items are classed as (4) ___'s. Not urgent and not important are classed as (5) ___'s. Not urgent but important are classed as (6) ___'s. We then take the A's and rate the most important one our (7) _____. Our next most important one becomes (8) _____ and so on. We do the same with our C's.

Our (9) ___'s (important but not urgent) are best listed separately on a (10) _____ objectives list. Each of these key tasks should have a (11) _____ opposite. At the appropriate time in the month, we then move them across onto our (12) _____ plan, when they become one of our (13) ___'s. Once we have listed and prioritised our tasks, we should start on the most (14) _____ one first and work through until it is (15) _____. There is always a danger of us spending so much time on (16) _____ tasks that we squeeze out the (17) _____.

A useful way to recall the nature of the ABCD categories is to remember the associated word. So, for instance: A is for Actioning, B is for (18) _____, C is for (19) _____ and D is for (20) _____. Provided we work through our tasks in (21) _____ order, it does not matter if we do not finish (22) _____ on our list. At least we will have been working on the most (23) _____.

When someone asks us to do something during the course of the day, be it the boss or a colleague, a useful question to ask is 'When do you (24) _____?' This will help us to (25) _____ it in the context of the work we already have to do. So, not Stimulus → Response, but Stimulus → (26) _____ → Response.

Owls are best (27) _____ in the day, whilst larks are best (28) _____. Whichever we tend to be, we should match our best time to our (29) _____ work. One of the dangers of working (30) _____ hours is that we may not be at our best at these times.

(31) _____ time is time we have put aside for a particular task or activity. However, we can often use this time productively. For instance, we can use travelling time in a variety of ways, provided we (32) _____ beforehand. It is usually best to plan the day in the (33) _____ rather than in the (34) _____. This enables the (35) _____ to be working on issues or challenges in the meantime. Mixing personal tasks with business tasks on your "To Do" list is a (36) _____ idea because it (37) _____ stress.

ANSWERS

(1) To Do (2) prioritise (3) A (4) C (5) D (6) B (7) A1 (8) A2 (9) B (10) monthly (11) deadline (12) daily (13) A (14) important (15) finished (16) urgent (17) important (18) Building (19) Curtailing (20) Ditching (21) priority (22) everything (23) important (24) need it by (25) prioritise (26) Think (27) later (28) earlier (29) important (30) extended (31) Committed (32) prepare (33) evening (34) morning (35) subconscious mind (36) good (37) reduces

SUMMARY OF SESSION THREE: Planning The Day

1. Write a daily "To Do" list. Start on the most important task first and complete each task before you go on to the next.
2. Prioritise tasks and do not let the **urgent** squeeze out the **important.**
3. Keep your important monthly objectives and milestones on a visible separate list and include them in your daily planning during the month.
4. Do not over-plan and be sure to expect the unexpected.
5. Plan and look for opportunities to use committed time productively.
6. Ideally, plan the day the night before, and write down all tasks, including personal ones, in one place.
7. Be both **efficient** and **effective** by focusing on the 20% of work that will give you 80% of your results.

If you want something to happen you must make time and space for it. Anon

Session

4

Session Four: Personal Time

By "personal time", I mean time spent working alone rather than with other people. The latter we call "people time" and will cover in the next Session. In this Session we will look at:

1. The story so far.
2. Managing interruptions.
3. How to say "No" and keep the job!
4. Being assertive, not aggressive or passive.
5. Saving time in solving problems.
6. Managing your health and stress.
7. Procrastination -- why we put things off and what to do about it.

1. The story so far

In the previous Sessions I suggested several ideas that can have a big impact on the quality and output of your personal time such as:

- Blocking "You" time in your diary to ensure sufficient time is available for you to work on **your** important tasks and projects.
- Matching this important work to your personal energy cycle to match quality time with quality tasks.
- Prioritising work in an urgent-important matrix of A, B, C and D.
- Starting and finishing the most important task first, before moving on to the next.
- Lessening the tendency towards procrastination that we all have, by following this prioritising approach.

However, this can be blown apart if we allow our day to become fragmented with interruptions. Indeed, constant interruptions were the top pressure felt by managers in the 2000 Taking the Strain survey by the (now) Chartered Management Institute (CMI) and AXA/PPP. According to an American survey, the average business owner may get one

> Unless we have ways of planning, scheduling and defending sensible blocks of uninterrupted time to work on our most important A and B tasks, we will either underperform or overwork.

interruption every eight minutes, lasting an average of five minutes, and accounting for four hours a day. Three of these hours were considered wasted due to the low value of the interruptions. It is difficult to have any continuity of thought in this environment.

Therefore, unless we have ways of planning, scheduling and defending sensible blocks of uninterrupted time to work on our most important A and B tasks, we will either underperform or overwork. So let us look at some proven ideas and techniques that might help you not to eliminate, but at least manage, your interruptions.

2. Managing interruptions

We will cover fifteen ideas under ten main headings, beginning with…

1. Red Time-Green Time

This particular idea has been around for a long time. For some companies, departments and individuals it works remarkably well. In other cases, due to poor implementation, it has been a disaster. Let me explain, starting with the basic traffic light stop-go idea.

- **Red Time** is time when you would prefer not to be disturbed.
- **Green Time** is time when you are available for colleagues and anyone else.

The key benefits and principles of Red Time-Green Time are:

- Spells of interruption-free time enable you to get more done in less time.
- In turn, this enables you to deliver better service to your colleagues at all levels and be more attentive to their needs when they see you.
- Red Time can especially be used for working on your B tasks. You can use it as thinking time. Reflect on what has happened and draw out the learning points or think about some intractable problem or new project.
- Red Time is that part of your planned important work in which you work by yourself. Other parts of your planned important work might involve working with other people, attending a meeting or making a site visit. But in Red Time you are on your own.
- It is only taken in limited blocks of time – usually one to two hours at a time. Some people are able to manage the odd half-day or even longer by agreement, whilst others have to settle for half an hour's Red Time. However, one to two hours per day is a good guideline.

Here are the Top Ten most frequently asked questions about Red Time:

1. **In my job I need to be available all the time, so Red Time cannot work in my case, can it?**
Your constant availability is a myth! You already have times when you are not available. For instance when you are in meetings, having your appraisal, speaking to someone else or having a day's leave. If this is true, then surely you can manage an occasional hour for Red Time.

Even if you're in a support role such as a technical expert, you still may be able to use the idea by for example:

- Arranging like-for-like cover with a colleague.
- Agreeing a "closed for enquiries hour" to coincide with a quieter period of the day (if you have one).
- Selling the concept to colleagues on the basis that it will ensure you keep on top of the requests for help that they make, resulting in better overall service.

Red Time is time when you would prefer not to be disturbed.
Green Time is time when you are available for colleagues and anyone else.

2. **What if something urgent crops up? People need to be able to contact me then.**
I agree. And although we usually frown upon interruptions to meetings or interviews, if something genuinely is urgent, then of course people need to be able to speak to you. However, you do need to agree a definition of urgent. So many so-called "urgent" matters can wait an hour or two until a meeting or Red Time has finished. Try to get a common understanding with immediate colleagues and, where possible, people who may call you. For instance, one organisation I worked with had a 4,000 miles test. To anyone who wanted to interrupt because they thought something was urgent, they were asked 'If Helen (or whoever) were 4,000 miles away in Head Office, would you still want to contact her?' That usually made people think and, very often, the query then seemed less urgent.

Someone who was waiting in reception at a retail customer's Head Office gave me another example. 'I only heard one side of the conversation from the receptionist,' he said, 'but it went something like this':

> Receptionist: 'No I am sorry he is not available right now. Can I take a message?'
> (Pause)
> Receptionist: 'How urgent?'
> (Pause)
> Receptionist: 'Well, let me put it this way. Has your store burnt down?
> (Very short pause)
> Receptionist: 'Then it is not urgent!'

3. **We are very team-oriented. If I said that I was not available to a colleague, they would see me as unco-operative. How do you get round that?**
Education is the answer. Certainly, just to implement Red Time without explaining your reasoning is a certain way to kill off the concept in double quick time. On the other hand, explaining the reasons behind your actions will ensure a better hearing. This is especially true if you point out the benefit to them. If you are on

top of your work, they are much more likely to get a better service. Think also of the Pareto Principle mentioned earlier. Who are the 20% of people who give you 80% of your communications? Ensure that this key 20% understand the whys and wherefores of what you are doing.

In summary, stress that your Red Time is designed to help the team, not hinder it.

4. **How will people know I am in Red Time? If I have to tell them every time, I am still getting the interruptions.**
    Once you have explained the concept, consider some signalling device. If you are one of the dwindling number of people who still have their own office, it is easy. A closed door indicates Red Time; an open door means Green Time. At least one blue-chip company uses red baseball caps – when you want some Red Time you pull on a cap. It has been established for some time and obviously works for them. However, if the very idea is at odds with your organisation's culture or your own personal style, try something else. Be creative, keep it simple, and above all make sure those around you understand what your Red Time is all about.

5. **Suppose other people like the idea and lots of people want Red Time. Will it still work then?**
    It certainly can do. The more people who understand the concept, the more likely it is to work. Key requirements are mutual respect and restraint in use. If an individual or department is continually unavailable, Red Time gains a bad name. This can obviously lead to pressures from on high to ban it. So, seek to ensure that any abuse of the system by a few does not jeopardise the improved productivity of the many.

6. **If it is that good, should we have a blanket Red Time for the department?**
    That depends. I know of some companies where the department's head has adopted it, explained it to staff and colleagues alike, and it works very nicely. Often there is one person on duty fielding any telephone calls and explaining that someone will get back to the caller within a pre-agreed time span.

    Equally, I can recall one very large organisation where it didn't work. The Senior Executive loved the concept and thought his birthday and Christmas had arrived simultaneously. 'Wonderful!' he exclaimed. 'Why don't we have Red Time for all directors from 9 to 10 every morning? Just think how much work we could get through if we were uninterrupted for an hour each day!'

    Unfortunately the body language of his colleagues betrayed some concerns. Eventually the Sales Director pointed out that his managers often liked to contact him around that time in the day and that a different time would be better for him. The Operations Director said the same, whilst the Finance Director said that he did not need any Red Time at all. Until the end of the month, that was, when he then wanted three days of solid Red Time to complete the month-end figures!

So, sometimes a blanket Red Time can work, sometimes it doesn't. This brings us back to the consultant's favourite comment, "it depends". See what is best for your team and then try and make it work.

7. **What about the telephone? I may be able to explain to people in my section, but I can still get interruptions on the phone.**
Most people now have a voicemail or other messaging facility on their telephone. These enable messages to be listened to at a convenient time, leaving Red Time untroubled by them. If you have it, use it.

It is especially useful if you also get into the habit of changing your telephone message. For instance, if you phone someone and get the message, 'I am sorry I am not able to take your call right now. Please leave your message and your number and I will get back to you', you are left with the question, 'Why can't they take my call and when exactly will they get back to me?' You do not know if they cannot get back to you because they are on a three-week holiday in the Bahamas, or in a two-hour meeting in the next office, or having a bit of quiet Red Time.

So why not change your message to something like, 'It's the 9th of May. I am in the building today, but cannot take your call right now. Please leave your message and contact number and I will get back to you by the end of the day.' I believe most people would find that acceptable, especially if you listen to all your messages and then call them back in priority order. Changing the message literally only takes about ten seconds to do.

8. **Nice try, but I haven't got voicemail.**
It is true that some organisations forbid voicemail as they always want customers' calls to be answered personally. If that is the case, can you divert calls to colleagues or reception? Get them to take messages and explain that you will call back today or within a defined period. Naturally, you will need to reciprocate for colleagues.

9. **Telephones are not the problem. I keep getting interruptions from emails.**
Do you remember the olden days when we first had faxes? I used to see whole offices come to a standstill and watch with wonder as a message would appear from the other side of the globe or from downtown Milton Keynes. 'Who is it from?' 'What does it say?' people used to ask as they crowded round this latest output of technological wizardry.

And would you believe it, this is happening again today in an office near you! The PC beeps or flags up that a new email has arrived and work stops. Some people just cannot resist seeing who is writing to them. 'Who is it from?' 'What does it say?' they ask, albeit to themselves. Such people are thinly disguised as email variants of chicken farmers. They allow their emails to manage their day. They drop whatever they are doing and allow every email to interrupt them. What's the answer?

Decide how many times a day you really need to look at your email. I find most people in most roles can manage on three times a day – first thing in the morning, around lunchtime and towards the end of the day. How might this suit you?

I have yet to meet anyone, even in the most reactive of jobs, who cannot let an email sit there for an hour or maybe two. Back to the earlier argument: if you were having an appraisal or were in a meeting, it would have to wait for you then. So, treat emails as potential interruptions. If you have not done so already, deactivate those annoying visual and/or audio reminders that you have new mail. Then look at your emails in batches when it suits you. Do not let emails get in the way of your productive Red Time.

10. I work in an open–plan environment where this simply will not work.
I understand the concern and it is certainly more difficult to operate when you do not have an office of your own. But notwithstanding the concern, there are thousands of people in open-plan situations like you that have made the Red Time idea work for them.

However, one other option to investigate is whether you can find a bolthole to hide in. Is there a meeting room or an absent manager's office where you can spend one or two hours away from your normal place of work? This is a growing need. A 2002 survey of 4,000 Management Institute members found that 46% expressed concern about the need for more office quiet areas. So if you have not got any, make the extra productivity case for having them.

Summary

The only way to find out if Red Time can work for you is to give it a try over a reasonable period. The first time I tried it, I was a closet Red Timer. I aimed for the principle of blocks of uninterrupted time without disclosing to people what I was doing and without mentioning Red Time. I worked on the principle that if pressed to attend a meeting in my Red Time, I was prepared to move, but tried not to remove my Red Time for the day. It worked surprisingly well.

The next interruption-saving ideas apply mainly to managers with staff who report to them. If this does not apply to you just yet, it may do one day, so why not take a quick look.

2. Weekly meetings

One way to reduce frequent interruptions from your own team is to schedule a short one-to-one weekly meeting with each team member. Get them to write down their queries gathered over the week and cover them altogether in one meeting. Obviously if there is something really pressing, then they will need to see you in-between meetings. However, in some offices, it is surprising how effective this simple idea can be for both parties. The manager has fewer interruptions. The direct report has a regular meeting and many of the issues resolve themselves beforehand anyway.

3. Bring solutions, not just problems

Do your people know the question you will ask them every time they come to you with a problem? Do they know that you will always ask, 'So what do you think we should do about it?'

The effect of consistently doing this is to make them think for themselves. Often they come up with the solution and so decide they need not interrupt you. If they proffer the right answer, they receive confirmation and a boost to self-confidence. In turn this reduces their need to interrupt. If they genuinely do not know what to do, an opportunity exists for development.

4. Coach and develop your people

By investing time in growing your people, you produce a confident, competent and motivated team. And confident, competent, motivated people have fewer reasons to want to interrupt you! We will look at methods of coaching and developing, as well as delegating, in our next Session on "People Time".

> One way to reduce frequent interruptions from your own team is to schedule a short one-to-one weekly meeting with each team member.

5. Be nicely direct

When someone does come into your office or to your workstation, how can you minimise the interruption? Essentially, be direct and to the point, but in a pleasant, acceptable way. John Adair puts it elegantly when he advises, 'be ruthless with time, gracious with people.'

For instance, which of these options is more likely to produce a quick outcome?

Option 1: 'Hello Andy, how are you?'
Option 2: 'Hello Andy, what can I do for you?'

You have it. Option 2 wins by getting straight to the point whilst being pleasant and helpful. Option 1 is an open invitation to hear about Andy's gripes, grievances or gossip of the moment. You will need to go through the resultant small talk before getting down to why he has actually come to see you. We will see in Session Five that this direct approach can also shorten phone calls.

6. Suggest a better time

Another approach, possibly in conjunction with the last one, is to suggest a better time. For business issues, perhaps something like, 'Yes, I am happy to go through that with you Andy, but I must finish this job before lunch. How is 2 o'clock for you?' For situations where someone has dropped in for a social chat, you may prefer to suggest lunchtime, or, if it really has to be in office hours, pick a time when you are at your least productive.

In all these scenarios, the aim is to maintain good working relationships with your colleagues, whilst minimising interruptions and facilitating a swift return to your priority task.

7. Stand up/No chairs

If you have your own office, standing up when someone comes in, and remaining standing, can communicate your wish that the interruption should not last long. This does not seem to work as well in an open-plan environment though.

A variant of this standing-up approach is the idea of perching on the edge of the desk. Again, this can work very well in some instances. However, it does not work in some cultures where sitting on someone's desk can be regarded as positively offensive!

Still on the standing-up theme, some managers have greatly reduced the length of unwanted interruptions by not having visitors' chairs easily available. Watching people surreptitiously looking for them can be quite entertaining!

8. Go to their workspace

If you are caught, shorten the interruption by walking over to their desk or office, rather than staying at yours. It is usually simpler for you to escape from their domain than it is to evict them from yours.

9. Appointment screening

If you have a personal assistant, secretary or colleague, seek their help in screening callers. Agree guidelines on who may see you at any time, such as your boss and other senior managers. Agree mutually acceptable ground rules with your direct reports on when they can interrupt you and when you would prefer they did not. Also agree the length of any Red Time and when you will be available to see people or call them back.

10. Flags and phrases

If finally, whether by invitation, insensitivity or misfortune, you are facing someone who is likely to interrupt your work longer than you would like, you may want to try out some of these flags and phrases.

A "flag" is when you flag up that there is a limit to how long you can spend with someone. The phrases are ones that can expedite a departure.

Flag examples (these are best used at the outset of the encounter for referring back to later).

- 'By the way, I have to ring a customer/colleague/supplier shortly, but we are OK for a couple of minutes...'
- 'Well, it is nice to see you again Sarah. I have to email this report before 3pm but I can spare a couple of minutes. Tell me how the new product was received.'
- 'I have to get ready for a meeting soon, but...'

All these flags enable you after a few minutes to say something like...

- 'Anyway, as I said, I have this ...to do/get ready for etc. I would love to talk with you more but at another time. Give my best to...' (Exit visitor with working relationship intact.)

Phrase examples

- 'And where are you off to from here? Who are you seeing next?' An old dairy farmer used to use this on me and it worked for him every time! Could you use it or some variant of it?
- 'Just before you go...' This is based on the tag line for a certain Scottish whisky. It signals the end of the discussion and allows a last topic before departure time.
- 'Anyway, I have to go now, so... (into summary of discussion and agreement of who is doing what, before a warm and cheery exit.) This works very well both face-to-face and on the phone.
- 'I'll let you get back to what you are doing.' This implies respect for their time and enables you to draw the conversation to a close.

All these flags and phrases are polite ways of dealing with interruptions.

Alternatively...

- If you know the interrupter very well, you may have the sort of relationship that enables you to sidestep all these gentle niceties without causing offence, by simply saying "Go away" or something similar.

This and all the ideas above, have all helped people reduce the number of their interruptions significantly. The question now is which ones might work for you?

Interruption Action Plan

Check through the list of techniques we have covered. In the table below, tick those ideas that might work in your environment. Add any ideas of your own. Put start dates against those that you plan trying out in the next four weeks.

Managing Interruptions Technique	✓	Starting from...
1. Red Time-Green Time		
2. Use voicemail		
3. Divert calls with updated message		
4. Limit checking emails to ___ times per day		
5. Have weekly one-to-one meetings		
6. Bring solutions, not just problems		
7. Coach and develop your people		
8. Be nicely direct in asking what people want		
9. Suggest a time for people to call back		
10. Stand up to shorten an interruption		
11. Make chairs less inviting		
12. Walk with people to their desk or office		
13. Brief support staff to screen interruptions		
14. Try suitable flags and phrases		
15. Go away!		
16.		
17.		
18.		
19.		
20.		

The above techniques will help you reduce the effect of interruptions on the achievement of your key goals.

To improve your personal performance and productivity still further, there is always the most powerful time management tool in the whole wide world. It has two letters...

3. How to say "No" and keep the job!

Here is a cautionary true story about Ken. Only the name has been changed to protect the identity.

Ken was a very talented employee. He was so good that people from other departments used to ask him if he could help them. And he always said "Yes". At first he did great jobs for others as well as for his own manager. And his image and reputation grew. So more people asked for his help. And he always said "Yes".

But eventually things started to go wrong. He said "Yes" to so many projects that his workload grew and grew and eventually became unmanageable. No longer was he able to hit promised deadlines. No longer was the quality of his work consistently high. No longer could colleagues rely on him. No longer did he have a good name and image.

In the discussions that followed, it transpired that he always said "Yes" for three main reasons:

- He genuinely liked helping people.
- He did not want to upset people or let them down.
- He also felt that to decline a request was to imply that he could not hold down his job.

Ken eventually came to see that always saying "Yes" to any request inevitably resulted in his becoming overloaded, inefficient and stressed. He disappointed his former admirers. He had to learn sometimes to say "No". As do we all.

But it will doubtless go down like the proverbial lead balloon if you go back to the office and say, 'I have just read this time management book and the answer is "No," so what is the question?' Instead I offer you…

Guidelines for saying "No" in a non-career-threatening way

Start by thinking "Yes!" Have a "can do" mindset and be seen by the world and his wife as being a positive, supportive team player, always happy to help when you can. That sort of deserved image will get you a much more sympathetic hearing when you do have to say "No".

Do say "Yes" to tasks and requests that will help you achieve the objectives and targets by which you will be judged. Tasks outside your own area should not be dismissed out of hand. 'That's not in my job description' or similar refrains sound inappropriate in today's competitive marketplace. After all, more and more organisations are going down the multi-tasking, dual-role approach, where co-operation and flexibility are key requirements. So again, think affirmative. Provided you have established your "good egg" credentials in this way, we can now look at when and how you might need to say "No".

Say "No" when saying "Yes" would mean that you could not achieve your own tasks and objectives on time and to the standard required. If you have time to do your own work and help someone else as well – great! Just do it. But beware of gradually being drawn into a situation almost by chance, where you end up doing a lot of work which is not your responsibility and which stops you from doing what is. Rick fell into this trap.

Rick was appointed to his job providing technical helpline support to sales people and customers. Because he was technically minded, he found it quite easy to sort out colleagues' computer problems. Word spread and gradually Rick found himself helping an increasing number of people on PC and Intranet-related glitches.

This meant his being away from his desk for much of the time – which meant he was not there to give the technical helpline support he was primarily paid to do – which meant complaints about his not doing the job properly – which meant cries from Rick of 'There aren't enough hours in the day' – which meant that he ended up on a time management course. So watch it, or that could be your fate!

The remedy was that either he had to start saying "No" to this other work or to agree a role and responsibility change with his manager. Beware of similar creeping changes surrounding your work. Be ready to say "No". As to how to say it, some of the following approaches might work for you.

> Say "No" when saying "Yes" would mean that you could not achieve your own tasks and objectives on time and to the standard required.

1. **Point out what will suffer.**
   'I would love to do that, but if I do, there is no way I can finish my customer survey on time. Sorry I can't help with this one.'

2. **Suggest a later deadline.** 'I'd be pleased to do that, provided we can agree a later date for that market report you asked for. If you could live with that being ready by Friday instead of Monday, I can do this new task for you, no problem.'

3. **Suggest an alternative method.** 'Well, let's see. If someone else can do the data research, that would give me time to finish this project before my deadline and then, yes, I would love to get involved.'

4. **Ask for help.** 'Well, boss, I will need your help on this one. With what I have on at the moment, I can't see how I can fit it all in. Here are my current objectives and schedule. I think I have a full workload right now. What do you think?'

5. **Ask when they need it by.** 'I have agreed to get some work out for your colleagues by tomorrow, which means I won't be able to start this until afterwards. When is the latest you need it by?'

6. **Ask the umpire.** If you are in a support role and are being unfairly pressured by some people to drop everybody else's work and do theirs, ask your boss to intervene. 'Can you help me? Malcolm insists that I drop everyone else's work and do his. But I have already promised Jackie I would get her mailshot results analysed by tonight. Can you agree a prioritising method between you that you are all happy with and that you will all work to?'

So key factors that come through these simple approaches are:

- Be positive and helpful.
- Give reasons for refusals.
- Involve people, such as your boss, in joint problem-solving where appropriate.
- Do not be a doormat and do not accept unreasonable pressure.
- Learn to be assertive, rather than aggressive or passive.

Which leads us onto...

4. Being assertive, not aggressive or passive

This Session is about safeguarding our "personal time" so that we can devote time to focus on our own work, priorities and objectives. To help us do this, we have so far looked at:

- How to manage interruptions to protect our quality time for quality work.
- How to say "No" in an acceptable way, when saying "Yes" would prevent us from achieving our own goals on time.

Both managing interruptions and saying "No" require us to be assertive. If we are either aggressive or passive, we will have problems.

For instance, does aggressive behaviour in others bring out the best in you? How do you react when someone comes in heavy handed, insisting they have their way with a backing group of threats, raised voices, banging of desks and slamming of doors?

This sort of behaviour certainly makes some people feel aggressive in return. The position of the aggressor usually determines whether this hostility is out in the open or seething beneath the surface. In others, it can produce a very defensive response. Excellent, if you want to stifle creativity and co-operation. Excellent, if you want to switch people off and get less than their best.

And how do you react to passive or submissive behaviour? These non-assertive souls might at first generate some sympathy for never being able to decline work, never making a fuss and always putting up with being put upon.   But sympathy can eventually turn to irritation and a lack of respect can quickly follow. Passive people also seem fair game for some aggressive types. 'Behave like a doormat and I'll treat you like a doormat' seems to be their attitude.

The difference between aggressive, passive and assertive people starts with the difference in the way they think and their basic beliefs.

The aggressive person has a mindset of…
'I have rights, needs and ideas. You do not.'

The passive or submissive person has a mindset of…
'You have rights, needs and ideas. I do not.'

The assertive person has a mindset of…
'I have rights, needs and ideas. So do you.'

So assertiveness is about expressing your needs, wants, feelings and beliefs in a direct, honest and appropriate way. It is about straight talking. It is about standing up for your own rights without violating those of the other person.

But what image does the word "rights" conjure up in your mind? To some people, it spells confrontation and conflict. To some people, there has been too much emphasis on "rights" and not enough on the matching "responsibilities". Fear not! Assertive people exercise their own rights and are responsible in recognising and accepting the rights of others. As to what rights we are talking about, here are some examples of rights that we should all have.

- The right to express feelings, views and opinions.
- The right to be ourselves.
- The right to be different.
- The right to make some mistakes.
- The right to know what is expected.
- The right to know how we are doing.
- The right to be listened to, even if not agreed with.
- The right not to accept sub-standard work.
- The right to be consulted on decisions that affect us.
- The right to refuse a request and not feel guilty.

This is not an exhaustive list but it will certainly give you a flavour of what I mean. Holding belief in your rights helps you to hold your head up high, look people in the eye, and treat them with respect, rather than in awe or in fear. And to demonstrate what rock-solid ground you are on here, consider this:

All human beings are born free and equal in dignity and rights.
Article 1 of the United Nations' *Universal Declaration of Human Rights*

Assertiveness needs working at. Like time management, it is a lifetime skill. Sometimes we overdo the assertiveness and we come across as aggressive. Sometimes we simply do not want a confrontation or conflict, so we accept something by being passive. Remembering Peter Honey's observation that **'Behaviour breeds behaviour'**, the more assertive we become, the more confidence and respect we will generate both in ourselves and from others. In turn, this will make us more successful in protecting and managing our time.

The more assertive we become, the more confidence and respect we will generate both in ourselves and from others. In turn, this will make us more successful in protecting and managing our time.

Assertiveness Exercise 1

Let us just ensure that you can recognise an assertive, aggressive or passive response when you hear one. Read the following situations and responses and then tick the appropriate column. Compare your answers with those at the end of the Session.

KEY: G = aGgressive   A = Assertive   P = Passive

Situation	Response	G	A	P
1. You are discussing the date of the next meeting of a committee. You are keen to attend but find the date accepted by everyone else means that you will not be able to attend. The chair asks if the date is all right for everyone. You say:	'Well OK, as it seems to be fine for everyone else.'			
2. One of your people interrupts you when you are making an important call to a customer. You say:	'I'll be happy to answer your question after I have finished this phone call.'			
3. A subordinate is trying to arrange a meeting with you later in the day. She asks, 'When will you be back from lunch?' You say:	'When I get here.'			
4. A colleague has just produced a good set of objectives for his department. You would like his help in how to write up yours. You say:	'Those objectives you produced were very good. Will you be able to spend half an hour with me to help improve mine?'			
5. A member of staff tells you she is keen to take on more responsibility with some of the department's enquiries. You say:	'What on earth for? You know you are struggling to keep up with your present workload without taking on more.'			

Situation	Response	G	A	P
6. A fellow manager in another department has just written you into one of his people's Personal Development Plan to coach her on preparing a marketing plan. He has not consulted you. You say:	'What a cheek. Why didn't you ask me first? There's no way I can help. I'm up to my eyes as it is. She'll have to work it out for herself like the rest of us.'			
7. A subordinate has asked for time off to visit a sick relative at a time when the department is frantically busy trying to handle a seasonal peak of customer orders. You say:	'Well I hope I don't sound mean, but the director won't like you to take time off just now. I'm very sorry.'			
8. Your boss wants Phil, one of your team, to carry out a survey for her over the next couple of weeks. You would really prefer Suzanne, another member of your team, to do the work. You say:	'Well I'm not sure. Phil has just started on the Preston contract but perhaps he could be taken off that. Suzanne won't be so good at the Preston job but I suppose I could always help her out.'			
9. Your boss asks you to attend a meeting. The last time you went it wasn't relevant to your department and you do not want to go again. You say:	'I'm really busy this week with budget preparations. I don't think I'll have time to go.'			
10. Your boss has brought a job that she wants you to complete today. You rate it as being a lower priority than the other work you have. To do as she asks will mean letting down some of her colleagues to whom you have already made commitments. You say:	'I cannot do this right now without breaking promises to some of your colleagues. But I can certainly make sure you get it by lunchtime tomorrow.'			

Assertiveness Exercise 2

Think of a recent situation in which, on reflection, you were aggressive or passive rather than assertive. Reflect on this:

Outline what happened.

What did you say and do?

How will you deal with this type of situation in future?

5. Saving time in solving problems

The respected management guru Edgar H. Schein comments, 'In my own experience in solving problems and watching others solve them, by far the most difficult step is the first one – defining the problem.' Schein goes on to talk of the dangers of failing to differentiate between symptoms and their causes, and warns of the propensity of the average manager to shortcut the problem analysis stage in their anxiety to find solutions.

From this it can be seen that failure to analyse a problem properly can waste vast amounts of your precious time. Hence, whilst in Session Two we discussed SMARTER objectives and action planning, in this section we can look at a rounder model of the whole problem-solving process. There are a variety of models around but most of them have the same basic ingredients. So what is presented here is a synthesis of several of them in the form of a four-stage model: defining the problem, writing an objective, generating options and implementing a plan (see Figure 14).

1. Define the problem

A good starting point with any major problem is to write down what the problem **seems** to be – the apparent problem. Various fact-finding tools can then be used to unearth the **real** problem. The Total Quality Management literature is particularly strong on fact-finding and problem analysis tools, such as the Ishikawa cause-and-

Problem-solving model

4 Implement PLAN	1 Define PROBLEM
• Action plan (what, who, when). • Review progress. • Adjust and achieve.	• Apparent problem. • Fact-finding techniques. • Real problem.
3 Generate OPTIONS	2 Write OBJECTIVE(S)
• Brainstorm. • Build on ideas. • Choose best vs criteria.	• Is it SMART? • Success criteria. • Check it solves the problem.

Figure 14

'In my own experience in solving problems and watching others solve them, by far the most difficult step is the first one – defining the problem.'

Edgar H. Schein

effect or fishbone diagrams. Here we will use two quick and easy methods. One is the Kipling (of Rudyard rather than cake fame!) method. The second is the several-times-why probing method.

To illustrate the first technique, one organisation I knew had a problem of staff turnover. The apparent problem seemed to be pay, as most people said in their exit interviews that they were leaving the company for jobs with more money. The sales managers pressed for an immediate rise in salaries all round, supported by numerous competitors' recruitment adverts offering higher salaries. The company could ill afford these rises and opted for a more detailed analysis of the problem. Senior management used the Kipling method based on his *Just So* stories:

I keep six honest serving-men:
(They taught me all I knew)
Their names are What and Where and When
And How and Why and Who.

The dialogue went like this:

So **what** is happening?	There is high staff turnover.
Where is this happening?	In the sales force.
When did this occur?	Over the last year.
How did it happen?	Not sure. But we seem to have had more people leaving recently.
Why are they leaving?	They all say it's for better salary.
Who is involved?	Well obviously the sales people, their managers, and the people that set salary levels.
Similar probing continued and the second time around…	
Where is this happening – all the teams or just some?	After checking the records it was found that in four of the six teams staff turnover was normal – most of the losses were coming from the other two teams.
What can you see that is different in these teams?	On more detailed questioning, it transpired that one manager was new and had an abrasive management style, whilst the other manager was new to the industry and was trying to impose unsuitable methods on an experienced team.
So **what** is the real reason for high staff turnover?	Two new regional sales managers! (Subsequent contact with people who had left confirmed this. Quoting salary as a reason for leaving is a common non-confrontational option many people choose to give, especially if their own manager is doing the exit interview!)

Had the company gone ahead with the expensive solution to tackle the apparent salary problem, they might have pleased the sales team but there would have been no guarantee that staff turnover would return to normal. Identifying the real problem saved time and money and resulted in coaching and training programmes for the two managers involved.

From a problem of staff turnover, we turn to a problem of product training to illustrate the second technique, using "why" and other probing questions.

Probing Questions	Responses Produced
So what is the problem?	The sales force needs extra product training.
Why is that?	Because they are losing sales.
Why are they losing sales?	Because managers report that every time they accompany sales people, they see missed sales opportunities.
Why are they missing these sales opportunities?	Because they cannot answer customer questions quickly enough.
Why is that?	If they cannot answer the question themselves, they have to phone the Product Department from the customers. Sometimes the people are on another call and sometimes they have just transferred from another product, don't know the answer, and have to go and ask a colleague anyway. In which case there is no on-the-spot answer.
And why does this lose sales?	Because a competitor salesman might come along in the meantime, know the answer and get the business.
A product quiz found that, on average, the sales people could only answer 4 questions out of 10. If so, how many would sales managers like them to be able to answer?	9 out of 10. Nobody can ever be expected to know everything but if they could consistently answer 9 out of 10 questions, we will get more business.
So the real problem question is, 'How do we get sales people to answer 9 out of 10 questions in front of the customer?'	Yes.

The answer in this case was not product training courses – the apparent solution to the apparent problem. It was the production of a compact but comprehensive product ring binder that enabled the sales team to produce instant, accurate answers when with customers. They also averaged over 90% scores on regular product quizzes. This method operated effectively for over ten years but was only made possible by an accurate diagnosis of the real problem.

Used flexibly and with sensitivity, both techniques will help you to identify missing information and move from the apparent problem to the real problem.

2. Write objective(s)

When the real problem has been identified, sometimes a single objective will produce the necessary solution. In other cases more than one objective may be needed. For instance, whenever there is a problem of falling sales there is often more than one cause. Usual suspects include training, motivation, competitors, service and suitability of the product for the market. In such cases, separate objectives in some or each of these areas may be necessary to solve the problem.

We covered the writing of SMARTER objectives in Session Two. Success criteria can sometimes be simple and built into the objective. For instance a logistics director's objective might be: 'To open our new Midlands distribution centre on time, within budget and with a full complement of trained staff.' The director's success can be measured against time, money, recruitment and training outcomes.

> Having written an objective with measurable success criteria, the final task is to check that the achievement of the objective will solve the original problem.

However, some success criteria may need to be spelt out more fully. As an example, in the product training example quoted above, the actual objective for this project listed 20 separate criteria that all had to be met. These included the scope of the programme and who was to be included, the methods to be used, as well as how it was to be implemented and maintained thereafter. These criteria proved not only valuable in measuring success at the end of the programme, but also in providing guidance and focus during the planning stage.

Having written an objective with measurable success criteria, the final task is to check that the achievement of the objective will solve the original problem. So, in the falling sales scenario, if the only objective pursued was an increase in marketing spend, then, without tackling the other issues we mentioned, it will probably be a waste of time as well as money.

3. Generate options

Having defined the problem and the objective that will solve the problem, we now need to look at the best option as to **how** we might achieve the objective. If we settle for the first idea that comes into our head we may be missing a more creative and elegant solution. You are, therefore, encouraged to think of various options you might adopt. This can best be illustrated with a real example.

Your problem – Part 1

Think of a current problem you have to solve. During a timed three minutes, list in the box below various options on how you might solve it.

Personally, I never cease to be amazed by the creativity and blocks to our creativity we all harbour in our minds. Irrespective of our personal abilities, we can all improve our creative output if we take the brakes off our brain.

During this exercise, for example, did you think of ideas that you then dismissed as impractical or too expensive or not worthwhile? Most of us tend to think in this judgemental way, strangling some of our ideas before they have even hit the paper. This can be very costly. For example, in initial discussions on the product training problem mentioned earlier, when someone suggested a loose-leaf product information binder, it was immediately condemned as impractical, impossible to do, and too heavy to carry. Fortunately, we deferred judgement, a key factor in developing options and creative solutions to problems.

Another blockage can be expectations. If you only thought a few ideas were possible in the time maybe you did not try too hard, just as people thought a sub-four-minute-mile was impossible until Roger Bannister proved otherwise. Our environment can affect us, such as cramped or unpleasant working conditions, represented here by a small box to write in rather than a larger one. Ridicule, criticism, lack of encouragement and support all block our creative output. So too do our own mental blocks. Which brings us to the famous nine dots exercise. You may be familiar with the first version but maybe not the other two. Here they are, and you may want some spare paper if you need several attempts.

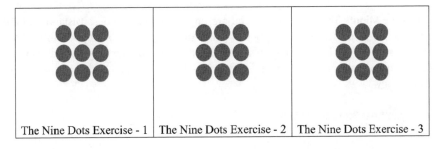

| The Nine Dots Exercise - 1 | The Nine Dots Exercise - 2 | The Nine Dots Exercise - 3 |

Nine Dots Exercise 1: Without lifting your pen from the page, connect all nine dots with no more than four straight lines, passing through each dot only once.

Nine Dots Exercise 2: This is the same as Exercise 1 but with a maximum of three straight lines.

Nine Dots Exercise 3: This is the same as Exercises 1 and 2 but with just one straight line (Yes, it is possible and there are several solutions!).

The only way to complete the exercise is to **think outside the box**, a term now gracing the pages of the Oxford English Dictionary as meaning 'to have ideas that are original, creative or innovative'. If despite this clue you still cannot remember or work out how it is done and if all else fails see the end of the Session.

After this gentle mental warm-up, let us look at some other pieces of equipment for our mind's gym, starting with brainstorming. This technique can be used individually or in groups and has some well-known rules.

1. **Defer judgement at first;** you can screen out the no-nos later. Immediate criticism will make people think before they speak and this will reduce the number of ideas offered.
2. **Off-the-wall ideas are welcomed.** They may be impractical but can often trigger other ideas that might work.
3. **Go for quantity not quality.** The more the merrier. It is easier to reduce a long list than expand a short one.
4. **Have fun!** A relaxed mind or atmosphere is more likely to produce winning options than a strictly serious approach.
5. **Build on ideas.** Ideas can often by improved or combined.

Brainstorming itself can be improved by combining it with other techniques such as alternating and creative questioning. You can try alternating between thinking and judging as just described, alternating between individual and group sessions, between short bursts and longer sessions and by changing viewpoints. Some useful creative questions are how might we… adapt, modify, magnify, minimise, substitute, reverse or combine. Enough of theory; it's time for more practise.

The Three Minute Tin Test: Imagine you are on an uninhabited desert island and the only thing you possess is an empty Coke tin. In the space above opposite, in three minutes, jot down how many uses you can think of for the tin. Remember the brainstorming rules: no judgement, crazy is fine, have fun, build and combine and go for quantity.

Can you beat 30 ideas in 3 minutes?

Over the years, I have heard well over a hundred different ideas in this exercise, showing the creative powers we all have when we unblock and unleash our amazing brains. Let us see if we can unleash some of your creativity on your own problem that you started in Part 1.

Your problem – Part 2

Taking the same current problem you used earlier, but using some of the brainstorming, alternating and questioning techniques discussed, how many options can you now come up with in a further three minutes that might solve the problem? One more time, the rules are: no judgement, crazy is fine, have fun, build and combine and go for quantity. Can you at least double your original options?

Having brainstormed and built on ideas to generate options, you now need to choose the best one. If this is not self-evident and clear-cut, measure each idea against a list of suitable criteria. Useful generic criteria to consider are **simplicity, acceptability, clarity, timeliness, suitability, feasibility, sustainability and cost-effectiveness.** A matrix of options versus criteria and a simple scoring system will often produce the best solution without recourse to more complex evaluation methods.

4. Implement plan

We covered action planning in Session Two, with the basic columns of **WHAT** has to be done, **WHO** is accountable for each action, and **WHEN** it is needed by, possibly split into start and finish dates.

In SMARTER objectives the E stands for Evaluated, where we check progress against the plan. Checking may identify the need to adjust the plan in some way. This is not surprising as our original plan is simply our best guess with the information available at the time. You may have noticed that sometimes things change! However, the advice is not to use this as an excuse for being late. Whilst sometimes it might be necessary to extend a finish date, very often such delays can be predicted, dates adjusted and the original deadline met.

Finally, you are not compelled to wait until a deadline for completion. Try finishing tasks and projects ahead of time when you can. It feels great, reduces stress and will further enhance your reputation. So please do not fall for the story put about by some people that they need the pressure of a deadline for them to perform. It is usually just an excuse by reactive people who get an adrenaline rush from being Lastminute.Tom.

6. Managing your health and stress

Talking of adrenaline brings us to the increasingly important topic of stress in the workplace, its rise and rise, and a three point plan to deal with it.

Pressure is not stress

Let us first differentiate between pressure and stress. Pressure in itself is not stressful but can become so. The relationship can be seen as a continuum as shown in Figure 15.

When pressure becomes stress

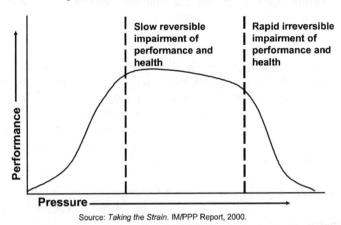

Source: *Taking the Strain*. IM/PPP Report, 2000.

Figure 15

We all need some pressure in order to perform. Without any pressure there is no satisfaction or sense of achievement. However, if the pressure becomes too great, there can be slow, albeit reversible, impairment in performance and health. If continued, this pressure becomes stress and can lead to rapid, irreversible deterioration of performance and health.

Today's workplace

The root source of much of this pressure is the need to improve international competitiveness. Successive UK governments have urged the British public and private sector companies to improve competitiveness by cutting costs and increasing productivity. A favourite way of cutting costs has been to downsize. This is an international trend, which for the remaining workforce usually means increased workloads, greater time pressures and longer hours. The 2000 CMI survey found that in the previous year, 69% of managers reported an increase in their workload. This rose to 76% where new technology was introduced and 77% where downsizing occurred. Two thirds of executives now have increased responsibilities.

Numerous studies show that the UK works longer hours than anywhere else in Europe. The CMI survey found that nine out of ten managers work more than their contracted hours, almost half regularly take work home, and four in ten work at weekends. The Chartered Institute of Personnel and Development's (CIPD's) *'Living to Work?'* survey found that the number of people working more than 48 hours a week rose from 10% in 1998 to 26% in 2003. Furthermore, the number of UK employees, especially managers and professionals, working 60 or more hours per week, rose from 11% in 2000 to 16% in 2002 according to the Department for Education and Employment (DfEE). Yet the Department of Trade and Industry (DTI) acknowledges that a long-hours culture results in stress and reduced efficiency.

From sources as widespread as Office Angels Recruitment, Teletext Holidays, the CIPD and several psychologists, it is evident that more than one in three workers fails to take their full holiday entitlement, whilst a growing number of people check their emails and phone the office whilst on holiday. A mixture of reasons is given such as wanting to impress or not let down the boss, guilt about the effect on teammates and the growing phenomenon of presenteeism. This is where people are afraid to take time off, either because they believe they are essential or because their absence will reveal they are not essential. Of those who claim they are essential to their work, psychologists say that for some of them, it is their work that is essential to them. For these individuals, their work defines who they are and affects their own sense of importance and self-worth. Difficulties at work can therefore have a disproportionately stressful effect on such people.

The human and organisational costs

Whilst some people claim to enjoy working long hours with no ill effects, the cost to many individuals is impaired health, with a greater likelihood of strokes and heart disease, damaged relationships and poor quality of life. A 2003 survey by Amicus for instance quoted long hours disrupting family life (45%), social life (38%), relationship with partner (35%), relationship with children (35%) and sex life (19%). The CMI found that 72% of managers have received criticism from family and friends about their long hours of work.

> It is evident that more than one in three workers fails to take their full holiday entitlement, whilst a growing number of people check their emails and phone the office whilst on holiday.

The cost of stress and long hours to organisations is also alarming. The Industrial Society found that stress was undermining the performance of 90% of companies, and 75% of employers saw stress as the most important workplace issue in the next few years. It is estimated that 25% of teachers, social workers and police officers are now suffering from serious stress. In other professions it is 10 to 15%. Many employees are taking early retirement because of the increased stress, causing chronic staff shortages in public services.

The Health and Safety Commission (HSC) figures for 2001-2002 estimated that 13.4 million days were lost due to stress-related illness, anxiety or depression: a figure that continues to rise, costing the country over £5billion a year. Another insidious cost is that of staff turnover. A 2001 survey for PeoplePC claimed that 10 million British workers would consider leaving their current jobs unless their employer acts to improve their work-life balance. With CIPD's estimates of recruitment costs at over £4,000 on average and over £6,000 for managers, the potential cost to employers is substantial.

Is this loss of staff likely or is it just talk? Well, consider the comments of Dr John Knell from the Industrial Society on the 2001 study, *'Willing Slaves? Employment in Britain in the 21st Century'*:

> 'Managers and professionals as a whole, and a fifth of new working graduates, are creaking under the pressure of longer hours and work strain. The magnitude of change captured by this survey over the last eight years suggests that we may be close to reaching a breaking point in the willingness of the UK workforce to tolerate the new deal at work.'

All the above paints a very bleak picture of increasing workplace pressure and its costs to individuals' health, relationships and quality of life. The measurable cost to organisations of absenteeism and staff turnover are compounded by the knock-on hidden costs of depleted and demoralised staff, delayed projects, and disappointing delivery of customer service.

Given the relentless pressures from the global marketplace, is this stress inevitable and just a fact of modern life, or can we do something to prevent or drastically reduce it? We believe the latter and present...

The three-step Stress Buster Plan

1. **Change your attitude to stress**
    The dictionary definition of stress is 'a state of mental or emotional strain or tension resulting from adverse or demanding circumstances' (Oxford English Dictionary). This implies that it is our circumstances that cause us stress, suggesting some inevitability.

    However, Dr Derek Roger of York University's Department of Health Sciences takes a different view. Author of *Managing Stress*, the first book in this CIM Skills In Action series, he argues that it is not our job or situation that causes stress but our **attitude** towards it. When inconvenienced by work or personal pressures, do we choose to allow these to further inconvenience us by producing stress? It is a choice we can learn to control with practise and Roger's book, based on many years of research and training, describes the techniques to deal with stress calmly, methodically and practically.

    This involves spending more time thinking in the present, rather than worrying "what ifs" about the future or "if onlys" about the past. Only then can you control your attention and take a compassionate but detached view of the potential stress. It also involves letting go of any encumbering baggage or hurt from the past. This approach of taking "a helicopter view" of looking down on a problem enables us to see things in perspective and separate the problem from the person. Yes, of course it takes practise, but the prize of less stress seems infinitely preferable to the inevitable outcome of prolonged stress, which is according to Roger "a short, miserable life". He is supported by these sample statistics:

'A landmark survey on the incidence of workplace stress in Britain, Germany, Poland, Finland and United States found that 1 in 10 adults suffered stress, depression and burnout.' UN's International Labour Organisation. *The Guardian*, 12 October 2000.

'Depression is the fastest growing epidemic in the UK. Currently, anti-depressants are prescribed 20 million times a year – a 700% increase in 10 years. It is estimated that in 20 years depression will overtake heart disease, Aids, malaria and malnutrition to become the commonest killer in the world after cancer.' Mental Health Foundation. *The Observer*, 7 January 2001.

'Burnout is now a recognised medical term. It diagnoses "chronic, work-related stress – the kind that even the most chilled weekend won't get rid of". The person feels incapable of coping because the demands put on him/her far exceed their ability to cope.' Corinne Usher, consultant clinical psychologist, Amersham Hospital. *The Sunday Times* Style 41 on health 2001.

All these challenges can be helped by constantly asking when problems arise **'Do I choose to allow or not allow this situation to stress me?'**

2.   **Control your time based on what is important**
One of the most common reasons for people to choose to come on a time management seminar is that they do not feel in control. Conversely, one of the main benefits people describe after training is seeing a way of overcoming the Chicken Farmer Syndrome and taking more control of their time and their life.

Most of the methods we have spelt out already – planning ahead, planning and prioritising the day, spending more personal and professional time on what is important at the expense of the less important, and the use of the "No" word. Other ideas on delegation, meetings, paperwork and emails are to follow.

> All these challenges can be helped by constantly asking when problems arise 'Do I choose to allow or not allow this situation to stress me?'

At the end of the book there is a "Stress Reducer Exercise", summarising the ideas contained in this book. You are asked to identify how many of these might contribute to helping you reduce stress. Seminar participants invariably rate "all or most" of the ideas as small potential stress reducers. Taken together, good time management ideas provide powerful stress-relieving medicine.

3.   **Promote an organisational Work-Life Balance culture**
The DTI-led Work-Life Balance campaign is heartening for those of us who believe in life after work. It encourages employers to provide more flexible arrangements for a better fit between work and home, and to create a climate in which people are motivated and enabled to work more effectively.

Whilst earlier we painted a picture of today's globally-pressured workplace, we now need to balance the equation with a picture of today's balance-pressured workforce. Most workers at all levels have a tough juggling act to satisfy some combination of work, home, garden, elderly parents, young children, teenagers, shopping, cooking, laundry, housework, friends, pets, partner, interests, commuting, socialising, career, training, qualifications, continuing professional development, email, voicemail, computer software, DIY and oh yes, holidays. Is it any wonder that today's workforce is under mounting pressure?

Given the comments earlier about the UK workforce reaching breaking point, a strong business case is made by the DTI and others for the benefits of offering a more flexible approach to employment to facilitate better work-life balances for staff. This is about offering people more control over their working time to fit in with the rest of their lives outside work. Considering that a DTI-Management Today survey found that more British workers would rather work shorter hours than win the lottery, it deserves senior management's careful consideration.

Contrasting with the stress-ridden problems described earlier, the reported benefits of work-life balance policies include motivated staff, the retention of valuable people, reduced absenteeism and increased productivity.

If you personally feel your organisation could do more to reduce stress and improve work-life balance, why not make one of your "B" important but not urgent tasks to make a proposal to investigate the economic benefits of more flexible working arrangements. Apart from the statistics given here, you can find more supporting information from the following web sites: www.employersforworklifebalance.org.uk (run by The Work Foundation – formerly The Industrial Society) and   (for research and practial tips) www.worklifebalancecentre.org.

If you have always meant to do something like that, but never got round to it, maybe you need to read the next section. No, please don't leave it till later...

7. Procrastination – why we put things off and what to do about it

Taken from the Latin, meaning "deferred till the morning", procrastination is a condition that affects all of us to varying degrees. We can all be extremely creative in finding excuses as to why we have not tackled a task we find unpleasant whilst finding time to do other tasks we enjoy. The frequency of our procrastination can therefore be somewhere on a continuum from seldom to serial.

Let us see where you sit on that line by looking at common symptoms of putting things off. We can then look at the costs, causes and what you can do about it.

Procrastination symptoms

As well as simply putting off doing a particular task, other common symptoms of procrastination include:

- Difficulty in **starting tasks**.
- **Seeking diversions** in work such as checking emails as they arrive, welcoming interruptions, phoning friends and colleagues.
- Spending a lot of time working but with **little to show** for it.
- Completing work in a rush at the **last minute**.
- **Missing deadlines** for the return of forms or reports or requests.
- Feeling **guilty when relaxing** rather than working.
- Arriving **late for meetings** and social engagements.
- **Miscalculating how long** things take, from car journeys to projects.
- **Blaming outside events** or other people for being late.
- **Keeping busy** with any jobs to avoid doing a specific job.
- **Anxieties** as discussed shortly.

Procrastination costs

We all know how it feels when we keep putting something off till the eleventh hour. It usually means that we worry about it for eleven hours and then have to do it in the twelfth hour anyway. Yet that is a minimal cost. At the other end of the spectrum, Neil Fiore, author of *The Now Habit*, a book specifically about procrastination, describes a vicious circle of people being overwhelmed, feeling pressure, fearing failure, trying harder, working longer, feeling resentful, losing motivation and so procrastinating. Not only do some people get trapped in this cycle, but also their misery is compounded by their feeling unable to enjoy leisure time without feelings of guilt at not working.

> We all know how it feels when we keep putting something off till the eleventh hour. It usually means that we worry about it for eleven hours and then have to do it in the twelfth hour anyway.

Some procrastinators hit their deadlines but at great personal cost and stress to themselves in terms of hours and energy expended. Others not only distress themselves but also inconvenience other people. These people are predictably late for meetings, ill prepared when they get there, and often fail to action their part of the minutes or provide colleagues with the data they need, when they need it. Their last minute approach to tasks makes them more likely to make mistakes (especially if they work late to catch up, when they are not at their best). In short, they fail to perform as well as they might.

Where procrastination results in delay, it can have a damaging effect on customer service, image or competitiveness. Add to that Victor Kiam's observation that 'Procrastination is opportunity's natural assassin' and it can be seen that procrastination can be costly all round.

Underlying causes

Fiore's definition of procrastination takes us to its root cause: **Procrastination is a mechanism for coping with the anxiety associated with starting or completing any task or decision.**

Examples of such anxieties Fiore cites as:

- Low self-esteem, involving lack of confidence and non-assertive behaviour.
- Perfectionism, often involving unrealistically high standards.
- Fear of failure, which in the case of perfectionists can mean even the most minor criticism.
- Fear of success and what that might bring. If we keep being successful, we might be promoted or otherwise given more challenging responsibilities, thereby increasing the risk of failure.
- Indecisiveness, often with difficulties of where to start or what method to use.
- An imbalance between work and play largely due to the guilt associated with play if work has been put off and still needs to be done.
- Ineffective goal-setting causing lack of direction, values, aims and little sense of what is and what is not important.
- Negative self-talk about work and self. If we tell ourselves often enough that we are "stupid" or "useless", the self-fulfilling prophecy comes into play, as does Henry Ford's dictum that 'whether you think you can or think you can't – you're right.'

Resentment sometimes plays a part. Perhaps we drag our feet because we dislike the person who gave us the task, or feel that no one ever reads the report we have been asked to do, or believe the application form we have to complete is badly designed and far too time consuming.

To these psychological issues can be added anxieties stemming from a lack of knowledge or skills in such areas as time management, problem solving, presentation and relevant technical subjects.

Every person on the planet shares the need for a feeling of self-worth. Therefore, any task that threatens to overwhelm us, or lead to failure, or trigger any of the other anxieties listed above is a threat to our self-worth. Procrastination is, therefore, a coping mechanism in these circumstances. It allows us to avoid the threat by putting it off. Not only that, it can have built-in rewards. For instance, we might postpone doing something, only to find that needs have changed and the task is no longer needed. As well as delay removing the anxiety, it now also rewards us with a feeling of justification. All such experiences tend to reinforce the "put-it-off" instinct.

Fortunately, whilst procrastination can become an ingrained habit, it is reversible. There are numerous tried and tested ways to help overcome it, several of which we have already covered.

> 'A journey of a thousand miles must begin with a single step.' Lao Tzu

Procrastination therapy – eight proven remedies

1. **Vision-to-action cycle**
    In Session Two, we saw the benefit of knowing where we are going in order to draw up objectives to help us on the way and determine our priorities on a monthly and daily basis. Coupled with the "Importance Exercise" in Session One, this will help overcome the ineffective goal-setting concerns.

2. **Macro and micro action planning**
    Following the vision-to-action cycle, we spoke of using start-line focused as opposed to deadline focused action plans. This involved breaking down our SMARTER objectives into more digestible chunks. For this, I normally recommend the use of high level or **macro** action plans. These answer the question "who has to do what by when?" and can fit easily on one sheet of paper. However, frequent procrastinators still find this size of project indigestible. It is too large and fails to overcome the feeling of being overwhelmed. They need to have the chunks reduced to a micro level of activity.

    For example an objective "to complete staff appraisals" might have a macro action plan with steps such as: agree dates, complete preparation forms, hold discussions, finalise forms, produce training plan and follow up. If these steps still feel overwhelming, then put them through an action plan "mincer". A useful one is David Allen's question in *Getting Things Done*, 'What's the next action?'

Using this mincer on the first step, to agree dates, it can work like this:

Q. What's the next action?
A. To contact my team members.
Q. So what's the next action?
A. To phone people.
Q. So what's the next action?
A. Start phoning.

Thus an overwhelming project has been reduced to starting with a few simple phone calls. It is an approach summarised by the ancient philosopher Lao Tzu when he famously wrote, 'A journey of a thousand miles must begin with a single step.' Now a single step is not overwhelming is it? So just take a step at a time.

3. **Choose your priorities**

In Session Three, you were introduced to the important/urgent matrix and the notion of starting the day with eggs before rice. You were encouraged to prioritise your eggs on the basis of importance. On the other hand, several writers advocate prioritising on the basis of difficulty. Get the most difficult job done first and you can enjoy the rest of the day they say.

Personally, I still advocate the importance criteria as the better one. Spending more time on what is important to you is the main thrust of this book. I would only do the most difficult task first if that happened to be my most important one as well. However, one pressure procrastinators can do without is being told prescriptively what they "ought" to do. We shall soon be advocating "choosing to" rather than "having to" as a more helpful approach.

Hence here, whilst I recommend you prioritise your day on the basis of importance, I believe it is more important that you choose the method that you feel is best for you. Time management is about guidelines, not tablets of stone. You have seen the options and now it is your choice.

4. **Reduce interruptions**

By using the techniques we have already discussed in this Session you will be able to focus on tasks rather than be easily distracted. If you find this difficult, think small. Aim for say just 30 minutes of uninterrupted time, or even less if necessary, before having a break and a reward of some kind for your efforts. Repeat the exercise a few times and you will soon start replacing your fears with some quality, finished tasks.

5. **Reduce the workload**

If you feel overwhelmed by the amount of work you are being asked to do, remember the discussions earlier in this Session on techniques for being assertive and saying "No". Delegation, which will be covered in the next Session, is another way of reducing the workload effectively whilst not losing control.

6. **Declutter**

In Session Six we will look at the benefits of working with a clear desk and having a bin bag day to rid your workspace of all the clutter. We will also look at how to establish a simple filing system that will enable you to file and retrieve items quickly and easily. All this, and ways of removing any backlogs of work, will unclutter your brain and help you focus on the task in hand. This will then look much less daunting.

7. **Mind map or brain dump reports**

If submitting quality reports on time is a dream rather than a reality, Session Six will also explain how to write reports and letters much faster using mind mapping or brain dumping techniques.

8. **Reprogram your self-talk**

'You can't do maths can you?' said my primary school teacher as my fourth attempt at an exercise was marked with a cross not a tick. Well, teacher said I couldn't do maths, so she must be right. Consequently, throughout the rest of my primary, junior and secondary schooling, whenever I was presented with anything mathematical, a large steel shutter came down in my mind with continual background self-talk that 'I can't do maths.' Subsequently, despite a brilliant teacher, I duly failed my maths exams. Yet years later in business, when I needed to work out profit margins, predict cash flow forecasts and balance a cashbook, there was not a problem. It was evident to me only then that for years I had suffered from my own ill-informed and damaging negative self-talk.

Similarly, frequent procrastinators often have damaging self-talk. Fiore has identified several variations, all of which need reprogramming to break out of the procrastinating mode. We have already spoken of breaking overwhelming tasks down into smaller ones by changing 'this is too big for me' to 'what's the next action?' Here are four more examples where reprogrammed self-talk is needed:

- **Should do to Choose to:** Constant 'I have to's' or 'I should be's' imply that there is no choice. The resultant inner conflict can produce stress or depression and diminished energy for the task in hand. Procrastination is the likely outcome. Changing "have to's" and "should do's" to 'I choose to' or 'I choose not to' can eliminate the conflict and the obstacle.

- **Future to Present:** If our self-talk emphasises "finishing" a task, as this is future oriented, it can detract from the present. Hence better to focus on 'what can I do now on this project.'

- **Perfection to Human:** Perfectionists tend to tell themselves that they must be perfect and not make mistakes and invite procrastination to save them from criticism. We spoke in Session One of Churchill saying that perfection spells paralysis and Fritz Perls commented, **'Friend, don't be a perfectionist. Perfectionism is a curse and a strain.'** Perfectionists among us therefore need to learn to change their 'I must be perfect and not make mistakes' self-talk to 'I am human and mistakes are ways of learning to be better'.

- **Guilt to Leisure:** Some procrastinators claim they must work on the project of the moment and have no time for leisure or the rest of life as we know it. When they do play they feel guilty. Changing the self-talk to insist 'I must make time to play, to go out with friends and family, enjoy leisure pursuits and take my holidays', will produce a more rounded person and increase the self-esteem that procrastination was being used to protect.

So listen out for any negative self-talk. Follow the example of leading sportspeople who use positive self-talk and positive images to help them perform to their peak.

Summary

Procrastination can be a major barrier to the effective use of our time, but understanding its cost and underlying causes, and applying the suggested time management remedies, can help to progressively reduce that barrier. In the process, we will gain more satisfaction from our work and a greater enjoyment of our play.

Suggested Answers To Assertiveness Exercise

1 P. 2 A. 3 G (If you have something different, it may be due to the tone or manner in which it was said. This can affect how others perceive behaviour. But in this example, said in an abrupt, throw-away manner, the response is certainly unhelpful to the questioner). 4 A (Giving and receiving compliments in a straightforward way is typical assertive behaviour). 5 G. 6 G. 7 P (Hiding behind the director is not being assertive. It is designed to avoid confrontation). 8 P. 9 P (Again, this is not giving the real reason why you do not want to go). 10 A.

The Nine Dots Exercise

Exercise 1
Starting with the top left dot, draw a straight line passing through the top middle and top right dots, but continue in a straight line for a short distance, thus travelling "outside the box" of the nine dots. For the second straight line, move diagonally through the middle right hand dot and the middle bottom dot, again continuing in a straight line until level with the left hand row of dots. For the third line draw vertically up through all three left hand dots. Finally, for the fourth line, travel diagonally down, passing through the remaining central dot and the bottom right hand dot.

Exercise 2
Starting with the top of the top left dot, draw a straight but slightly sloping line passing through the middle of the top middle dot, the bottom of the top right dot and out to the right-hand side. For the second line, repeat the straight but slightly sloping character, this time passing through the top of the right hand middle dot, the middle of the central dot and the bottom of the middle left hand dot. Once more, continue this line outside the box. The third line, also slightly sloping, can now pass through each of the bottom three dots.

Exercise 3
All nine dots can be joined together with a very wide felt tip pen. Alternatively, the nine dots can be folded one on top of the other and a vertical line drawn through them with a sharply pointed pen. There are several other options. All these answers depend upon not being bound by imagined constraints such as having to work within the nine dot box or having to use a particular type of pen.

SUMMARY OF SESSION FOUR: Personal Time

1. You will achieve most of your key results when you are working by yourself. Block this time in your diary to work on your priorities for each day.
2. Safeguard these blocks of "you" time with Red Time and other techniques.
3. Learn to say "No" in an acceptable way to prevent yourself becoming overloaded.
4. Be assertive rather than aggressive or passive, treating everyone with respect and earning the respect and co-operation of others in the process.
5. Save time by carefully analysing the real problem, before writing an objective, generating options and implementing a plan.
6. Safeguard your health by choosing not to be stressed, using good time management techniques, and promoting an organisational Work-Life Balance culture.
7. Reduce any tendencies to procrastinate by having clear goals and priorities, macro and micro action plans, fewer interruptions, less workload, less clutter, less negative self-talk and mind mapped reports.

Session

5

Session Five: People Time

Whilst it is important that we preserve some time to work on our own, most of us can only achieve our goals by working with and through other people. The people aspects we will look at in this Session are:

1. Working with the boss and the three choices you always have.
2. The boss's time template.
3. Multiplication by delegation.
4. The Better Meetings Campaign.
5. Communicate! Communicate!
6. Ensuring time management training is not a waste of time.

1. Working with the boss and the three choices you always have

If you and your boss like each other, and get on well together, it makes life much more enjoyable. However, you don't have to like each other, provided you have a professional, working relationship. For your part, there are several ways you can contribute…

Working Relationship Guidelines

1. Have a "no surprises" policy (that is, if you have a problem or make a mistake, tell your boss rather than letting them find out).
2. Communicate and present information and reports in the way your boss likes to receive them, as opposed to how you like to give them. For instance, with reports, some people prefer to receive numbers, whilst others prefer pictures, graphs and charts. Some people prefer the written word, whilst others prefer a more informal, verbal communication.
3. Be loyal to your boss in front of junior staff, even when you do not agree with them.
4. Treat your boss with the same consideration you would like from your own direct reports.
5. Seek ways to help your boss with their boss's priorities and projects. The more you can help your boss look good, the better it will reflect on you.
6. Present suggested solutions as well as flagging up problems.
7. Accept feedback graciously, be it good or bad. If it's good, a simple "thank you" will suffice. If it's bad, make sure you understand why and learn from it.
8. Walk the extra mile. Helping your boss out over and above the norm will strengthen your position when you want some flexibility for a special occasion.
9. Time requests, disagreements or new proposals carefully. When are you likely to get the best hearing? With some bosses any time is good, whilst with others good timing can be vital.
10. Behave assertively with your boss. This means never losing your temper, which can only lose you respect. It also means standing up for yourself on important

issues rather than allowing yourself to be walked all over. As mentioned in the last Session, assertive behaviour breeds assertive behaviour and will increase your boss's respect for you.

11. Finally, build up your boss's confidence in you by being reliable in doing what you say you will do. Make sure you do not overcommit yourself, and equally, with the commitments you do make, ensure that you deliver as promised.

Your boss and your time

From your viewpoint, your personal time management can be greatly affected for good or ill by your boss. Fortunately, most bosses understand that if they are to succeed they need their people to succeed. Consequently, they respect their people's time as they do their own. They seek to empower and enable their people to achieve good results by identifying and removing barriers to performance.

You will shortly have the opportunity to assess how good, bad or indifferent both you (if you are a manager) and your boss are on a number of measures. Right now, however, we will focus on what you can do if you are one of the minority who have a boss that is a disruptive influence on the way you try to plan and manage your time, especially your personal project time.

The three options

Throughout our lives, in any situation, there are always three options. We can try to **CHANGE** things, **ACCEPT** things or **LEAVE**! So, for instance, if we do not like the way the boss operates in disrupting our day, we can try to change things. Happily nowadays most people can do this. Most people seem to have a good, open relationship with their boss, where they can sit down and have a professional one-to-one discussion about any problems between them. For this majority, there is no problem.

But for those who cannot seem to change or even influence the actions of their boss (and the negative impact they can have on your time management), it's decision time! If, despite our best efforts, we cannot change things, then we may have to accept the situation. In this category, we all know people who accept things in different ways, namely:

Accepting real-world, unchangeable situations with a philosophical, 'that's the way it is, so I may as well just get on with it' attitude can save us an enormous amount of time and grief. It can be useful at such times to recall the Serenity prayer, first credited to Boethius, a sixth century Roman philosopher:

**God grant me the serenity to accept the things I cannot change,
courage to change the things I can, and the wisdom to know the difference.**

Here are a couple of further thoughts to ponder on, whilst you consider the options.

How important are the job, the income, the experience and so on, to you? We are back to the Importance Exercise you did in Session One. If the job and what it can give you are very important, then you may well have to accept putting up with your boss's foibles as part of the cost.

Whilst he or she may be a pain at times, is your boss good for the business? Sometimes, the drive, the passion, the vision, the industry knowledge or the flair of a boss, especially a senior boss, can be of real value to a business. If a downside is self-management or people management skills that are less than ideal, it may be a price the business is willing to pay, in which case, accept the shortcomings. Do not take things personally. Get on with life.

> A manager's support in a crisis and the paying of compliments were the most motivating actions a manager could take. Honesty, loyalty and the ability to both give and receive honest feedback separated the bad from the good manager.

Finally, if we cannot change a situation, are unable or unwilling to accept it with good grace, then we always have the third option, which is to leave! Remember though that a boss is not necessarily there forever. It may be that by staying in the job a little while longer your boss leaves before you do. Hopefully you will work hard on the change and acceptance routes first. But if all else fails – there is always the third option.

2. The boss's time template

A 2003 survey by specialist Human Resource Consultancy Cubiks found that ineffective managers are fuelling high staff turnover rates and widespread employee underperformance. At a time when more is being expected of managers themselves, this seems especially perverse. The report found that a manager's support in a crisis and the paying of compliments were the most motivating actions a manager could take. Honesty, loyalty and the ability to both give and receive honest feedback separated the bad from the good manager.

In this context, here is my guide to how good bosses can multiply their own time by retaining the staff around them and making them more capable and confident. The criteria I have used are an amalgam of various sources, not least the typical "good boss" feedback we get from delegates on courses. The yardsticks, each of which have time implications for you and your people, are summarised in Figure 16.

Good bosses make time for...

A greeing direction, objectives and priorities.

G iving enough time to listen and help.

R eviewing delegated work as needed.

E mpowering initiative and involvement.

E ncouraging by respecting people's time.

M aking decisions professionally and swiftly.

E xpecting and demonstrating high standards.

N etworking to keep people informed.

T rusting people and earning their trust.

Figure 16

Agree direction, objectives and priorities

One of the biggest time wasters for people is not having "the big picture" of where the organisation is going, what their own objectives are to help achieve this, and what the priorities really are. Remember that when everything is a priority, nothing is a priority.

Give enough time to listen and help

There are two extremes here. Some managers with an open door policy will see any of their people at any time. This is sometimes to the detriment of achieving their own tasks and can also generate a climate where people are not encouraged to think and act for themselves. At the other extreme is the boss who is so busy that he or she is never available to see team members. Then, when they do see people, some of them do not listen properly, or they promise help and do not deliver. Both examples would warrant a low score. On the other hand, a boss who will see you, always listen to you, and provide the level of help you need in different situations and still do their own work effectively, will score highly.

Review delegated work as needed

When we cover delegation, we will see the need to agree a suitable level of reporting on progress, based on the experience of the delegate and nature of the task. Some managers think they are delegating but fail to set up an agreed review arrangement. This then becomes abdication not delegation. Also, if review dates are set, they should be kept.

Empower initiative and involvement

By empowering people to make their own decisions within agreed guidelines and policies you free up the time of both boss and subordinate. In the process you unleash two powerful motivators – increased responsibility and involvement.

Encourage by respecting people's time

Some bosses act as though their people's time is just an extension of their own, to do with as they will. Such people will happily interrupt whatever their underlings are doing on the basis that it cannot possibly be as important as their own work. They would not dream of checking when they phone to see if it is a good time to talk. Nor are they averse to keeping people waiting. At the other end of the spectrum are considerate bosses. They demonstrate their respect for their people and their people's time in everything they say and do. In return, they earn the willing co-operation of their followers. Charles Schwab, mentioned in Session Three on planning and prioritising the day, was one leader/manager who won such co-operation from his people. One of his quotes echoes the findings of the Cubiks survey: 'The way to develop the best that is in man is by appreciation and encouragement'.

Make decisions professionally and swiftly

A major failure of poor managers is indecision. It is one thing to want to "sleep on it" or to want more information before reaching a decision. But if getting a decision out of a manager is like getting blood out of a stone, it can be very demotivational as well as hindering people in their work.

> 'The way to develop the best that is in man is by appreciation and encouragement.'
>
> Charles Schwab

Managers who give their people quick decisions win lots of friends. Provided, that is, that their decisions are seen to have been made in a professional rather than instinctive "shoot from the hip" way. So, do these good managers follow some sequence or plan in their decision making? They might use a very structured approach such as Kepner Tregoe, or a quality management-related method, or the four-step approach covered in Session Four. Or their decision making might be informal. If you prefer a shorter version, does it ADD things up?

- **A** nalyse the problem – if necessary by getting more information.
- **D** etermine the cause(s).
- **D** ecide the best option and be able to justify your choice.

Expect and demonstrate high standards

Are people clear on exactly what is expected of them? Is this demanding but achievable? Does the boss personally lead by example or is there a credibility gap?

Network to keep people informed

Does the boss network with colleagues and seniors so as to know what is going on and keep people in the picture? Not in a "mushroom management" way (tell 'em something once or twice a year and keep 'em in the dark in between), but in a regular, structured, consistent way, especially with information affecting the individuals concerned and their work. When bosses do not do this, how much time and energy is spent in needless speculation and pointless work?

Trust people and earn their trust

Bosses who trust people to make decisions and get on with the job within agreed guidelines and standards can save a lot of time for everyone concerned. The boss gets fewer interruptions from people seeking approval for this and that, and staff don't waste time having to wait for the boss's say-so. Trust breeds trust. And mutual trust is one of the bedrocks of productive teams.

Boss Assessment Exercise 1

Now it is assessment time. On the following table see how your boss scores on each of the measures. And if you are a boss yourself, see how you score. Better still, ask a few of your people to do it. It might give you some helpful insights into how you are perceived and how you might manage your team better. If you are not prepared to do this, why should your boss listen to your thoughts on them? Go on, be brave!

You	1 = Poor 5 = Excellent	Your boss
1 2 3 4 5	Agrees direction, objectives and priorities.	1 2 3 4 5
1 2 3 4 5	Gives enough time to listen and help.	1 2 3 4 5
1 2 3 4 5	Reviews delegated work as needed.	1 2 3 4 5
1 2 3 4 5	Empowers initiative and involvement.	1 2 3 4 5
1 2 3 4 5	Encourages by respecting people's time.	1 2 3 4 5
1 2 3 4 5	Makes decisions professionally and swiftly.	1 2 3 4 5
1 2 3 4 5	Expects and demonstrates high standards.	1 2 3 4 5
1 2 3 4 5	Networks to keep people informed.	1 2 3 4 5
1 2 3 4 5	Trusts people and earns their trust.	1 2 3 4 5

COMMENTS/ CONCLUSIONS/ ACTIONS NEEDED

3. Multiplication by delegation

I have no one to delegate to so this section is not for me. Wrong!

The good news is that you can develop your delegation skills by the way you receive delegated tasks as well as how you give them. It also applies to work you agree to do for colleagues and to work they agree to do for you. This section shows you how to develop your delegation skills and covers:

1. The vital importance of delegation.
2. What gets in the way of effective delegation?
3. A definition of terms.
4. What we can and cannot delegate.
5. The all-important how to delegate (and how to receive delegation) using the acronym TIARA:

T ask defined.
I ndividual identified.
A greement reached.
R eviews conducted.
A cknowledgement given.

1. The vital importance of delegation

Effective delegation often has a triple bonus. It frees up more time for the manager, saves them recruitment time by reducing staff turnover, and develops the delegate. As Booker T. Washington observed, **'Few things help an individual more than to place responsibility upon him and let him know that you trust him.'**

Look at your manager friends who do not delegate. They are the ones left working by themselves when all their people have gone home. They are the ones who take work home and see their golf handicap go up as their people's handicaps come down. They are the ones with disillusioned and bored people who feel they are not learning anything, not going anywhere, and so decide to go somewhere else instead. They are the ones who go through the pointless and time-consuming cycle of recruiting good people, only to abuse them by misusing them once they have got them. They are the ones who are always behind, have recurring problems that never get fixed, are late with work, worry about taking holidays, have no time for planning, and certainly have no time for delegating. Or so they say.

Poor delegation is one of the most common reasons for people being sent on a time management course. Poor delegation is rife though all organisations, big and small. But it needn't be so.

Effective delegation is a process that can be followed and a skill that can be developed. Even without experience or practise, just follow the process and you will make huge gains, time being only one of them.

> Effective delegation often has a triple bonus. It frees up more time for the manager, saves them recruitment time by reducing staff turnover, and develops the delegate.

2. What gets in the way of effective delegation?

Common reasons managers give for failure to delegate are fear, ignorance and attitude.

Fears are usually that:

- The job will not be done properly.
- They will get the blame when it goes wrong.
- The job will be done differently to how they would do it.
- It will not be done as well.
- Even worse – it might be done better!
- They will lose their unique expert status.
- Their people are overloaded as it is.

Ignorance is about:

- What can and cannot be delegated.
- How to delegate effectively.

Attitudes include:

- 'It's quicker to do it myself.'
- 'I haven't got time to delegate.'
- 'I had a bad experience once!'

It is easy to be dismissive of these concerns as being mere excuses. Sometimes they are. But equally, the fears, whether real or imagined, do exist in some managers' minds. Such people will hopefully find reassurance in research on delegation, which indicates that:

- People usually do a much better job than we expected.
- It is very developmental for them.
- They appreciate us delegating the same or similar tasks again in the future.
- It paves the way for delegating even more stretching tasks.

As Jan Carlzon, former head of SAS Airlines observed, **'You can get people to develop their skills not by steering them by fixed rules but by giving them total responsibility to achieve a specified result.'**

3. A definition of terms

There is often some loose and variable usage of terms such as responsibility, accountability and authority. So let us clarify my usage here.

Responsibility is the work that is assigned to a position. So, for instance, a human resource manager's responsibilities might include recruitment, training, health and safety, staff welfare, salary administration and so on.

Accountability is the obligation to carry out those responsibilities.

Authority is the rights and powers that go with a position. For instance, the human resource manager may be given the authority to determine salary levels. The sales manager may be given the authority to agree customer discounts.

Delegation is the work that managers do to entrust others with responsibility and authority and to agree accountability for results.

What does all this mean? It means that you can delegate a part of your responsibility to someone else. You can give them the authority to carry it out. You can make them accountable for producing an agreed result. But if it all goes pear-shaped, you cannot abdicate your responsibility and say 'It wasn't my fault.' You retain ultimate accountability, even when you delegate something, and so the famous President Truman motto applies to you – 'The buck stops here!'

So let us now focus on how we can reduce the risk of things going wrong, starting with...

4. What we can and cannot delegate

We can consider delegating:

- The **technical**, as opposed to management, parts of the job.
- Some of the **routine** tasks, especially the time-consuming ones.
- Some **meaty**, complete projects to the right person at the right time. And once delegated, we should only accept:
- **Finished** work, not half-finished and delegated back up to us!

Let us develop these points a little. In Session One, Figure 3, we pointed out that as we climb the managerial ladder, we should be doing less technical work and more management work. That being the case, the **technical** parts of our functional specialism are prime candidates for delegation. This will leave us more time for our management work of planning, organising, leading and controlling.

We can also delegate some **routine** parts of our job. Provided we explain that the reason for the delegation is to enable us to do other things, provided we explain why the work is important and provided we do not do it excessively, we should not hesitate. However, some managers do. They feel it is unfair to give their people boring, routine tasks to do. Well, firstly, if our people do not do it, we will have to do it. And secondly, what may be boring to us may not be boring to them.

For instance, one company I worked with had a policy of sales people phoning their manager mid-week during the early stages of any new product launch. It helped them to respond rapidly if plans were going adrift. However, it did mean that the sales managers had to be available each Wednesday evening and, after a few months, some of them found this a bore. At holiday time, they resisted delegating the task to one of their sales people. 'It's routine. It's boring,' they said. 'Too bad,' was the reply, 'we need the figures.'

To their amazement, when they returned from their holidays, their delegates were full of it. They enjoyed talking to their colleagues, swapping ideas and hearing who was selling what. A routine and boring task to the sales managers was a stimulating and novel experience for their teams.

> Which part of your job do you enjoy the most and can you delegate it?

As well as technical and routine tasks, consider **meaty** tasks. Now here is something to frighten you. I was once told to think of the work that I enjoy the most and to delegate that! The point was made that sometimes we hang onto something longer than we should, simply because we enjoy it. But in terms of the best use of our time, perhaps someone else could do it instead.

At the time, my responsibilities included organising the annual sales conference. I used to love it. It involved visiting the venues, using the latest audio-visual wizardry, knowing all that was going to be said, coaching the speakers. Great fun! But taking the advice to heart, I called in two of my people and delegated the whole conference to them. Seeing each of them grow from a disbelieving dumbstruck to an enthusiastic expert in a matter of months was a most rewarding management experience.

So I commend it and ask you the question I was asked – which part of your job do you enjoy the most and can you delegate it?

Finally in this section, we should require delegated work to be **finished** work. What do we mean?

> A new director asked one of his managers to get some information from another department. The manager returned empty-handed, saying that the information was confidential and would only be given to the director personally.

This is incomplete delegated work. It is so easy on these occasions to say, 'OK. Leave it with me.' However, to the manager's surprise, she was asked to go back and explain that the director was authorising her to collect the information on his behalf and this could be verified by phone if need be. She got the information. The director got the delegated work completed.

Be like that director. Do not accept unfinished business. After all, who is working for whom here? This idea is developed much more in Oncken and Wass's classic and amusing *Harvard Business Review* article, 'Who's Got The Monkey?', and in *The One Minute Manager Meets The Monkey.* Both are mentioned in the bibliography at the end of this book.

The authors use the analogy of a problem being like a monkey. Delegated problems or monkeys once accepted should not be allowed back onto the delegator's back. All requests for the manager to look after it should be resisted. By all means help them feed the monkey and solve the problem. But it should stay in the care of the delegate, not the delegator.

Finally, a word on what we **cannot delegate**:

- Specialist technical work that only we can do.
- Our final management decisions.
- Work that needs a broad company, rather than narrow departmental view.
- Some people issues – you can hardly delegate performance reviews or salary discussions!
- Ultimate accountability, even when responsibility to carry out a task has been delegated. Once again 'the buck stops here!'

5. How to delegate

The TIARA process can remind us of what to look out for when we delegate to others, or when we have things delegated to us. It also applies when we persuade colleagues to do some work for us or agree to do some work for them.

Task defined

We need to be crystal clear on exactly what is to be accomplished. Time spent on this aspect will be more than repaid by fewer misunderstandings later.

And, talking of timings, delegate **as soon as possible**. We heard in an earlier Session where people on the receiving end quite rightly see last-minute delegating as dumping. So, define the task to be done and delegate early.

Individual identified

If speed of completion is a factor, you may opt for someone who is experienced. But if you have a little more time to play with, think of using the delegation as a development opportunity for one of your inexperienced people. If this involves some training or coaching of the individual, either do this yourself or delegate it to an experienced person. In either case, make sure that you follow simple, sound training or coaching practice. For training, put the task to be learnt into context by giving the big picture before going into the detail. Split any big learning into digestible chunks. Follow the five-step training cycle shown in Figure 17. For tips on one-to-one coaching skills, try Julie Starr's excellent coaching manual listed in the bibliography.

The training cycle

PREPARATION – points to cover, props.

EXPLANATION – importance, aim, method.

DEMONSTRATION – how it is done.

OBSERVATION – delegate tries the task.

EVALUATION – feedback, encouragement.

Figure 17

Agreement reached

When you delegate a task, it is important to gain both understanding and acceptance. You can check that the delegate understands what is expected of them by getting them to summarise what they have to do. You can then correct any misconceptions. Without full acceptance of the task by the individual, there will be no motivation to complete it. So ensure they are ready, willing and able to undertake the task. Can they fit it in with their present workload? Explain why you have chosen them for the job.

Agree what level of help they will need. Do they need training or are they competent? Will they need additional resources of time, money or people? What authority will they need? Give guidelines and limits on all of these.

Finally, what level and type of progress reporting do you want? This leads us on to…

Reviews conducted

As stated earlier, without a review of progress we have abdication not delegation. But the level of reporting needed will vary according to the experience of the delegate, the nature of the task, and the amount of interest in it from the wider organisation.

Delegation control model

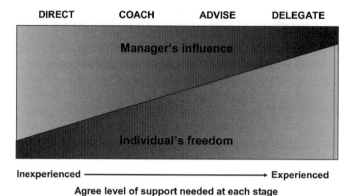

DIRECT   COACH   ADVISE   DELEGATE

Manager's influence

Individual's freedom

Inexperienced ————————————————→ Experienced

Agree level of support needed at each stage

Adapted from Hersey and Blanchard

Figure 18

From Figure 18 we can see that someone who is inexperienced in the particular work will need more of the manager's time than an experienced person. We can also see that having the same style of controlling for each level of experience is inappropriate.

Someone who has never done the work before will be quite happy to be directed as to what to do. But imagine how an experienced person would feel with this approach! From directing, the manager can move to a coaching style, where the work is discussed and the delegate encouraged and guided to come up with their own solutions. With further competence, only occasional advice might be needed. 'Have you spoken to manufacturing?' 'Have you got alternative costings?' and similar non-directive approaches. Finally, if someone is totally competent in the work, the task can be fully delegated, with the understanding that they will only come to you with a problem.

However, as you can see in Figure 18, there is still a manager's influence and control, albeit it much less than with some of the other scenarios. So decide the level, frequency and type of review necessary at all stages of a delegated task. Depending upon the circumstances, you might have anything from a regular meeting, to a monthly one-page report, to a less formal review process. But do arrange reviews and do have them. They are the best way of ensuring a "no surprises", low-risk delegating experience.

Acknowledgement given
When a delegated job is done well, say 'Thank you.' This is painless, quick and costs nothing. It is invariably appreciated and is a simple form of recognition, which in turn is one of the most powerful motivators. So acknowledge appropriately. A quiet, private word for a simple job, a public acclamation for a big project well delivered.

Delegation Exercise 1

Back to our readers with no one to delegate to – there are a growing
number of you these days. Perhaps this is your first appointment, or perhaps
you have a very senior but highly specialised role with only shared support
staff. Whatever your situation, you can develop your delegation skills by
going through the delegation process with your boss when they delegates a
task to you.

Think of tasks or projects you have had delegated to you recently. In each case ask
yourself:

TASK defined	– am I crystal clear about what is required of me?
INDIVIDUAL identified	– do I have the skills and knowledge for the job?
AGREEMENT reached	– have we clarified resources, timing, scope, authority – and reporting?
REVIEWS conducted	– are we reviewing progress sufficiently?

Delegation Exercise 2

Now what will you do? Will you do more delegating? Will you invest time to save
time? Will you put names and dates to tasks? And for your own development – are
there any tasks that you could do that would save your boss time and give you more
experience in the process?

Type of work to delegate	Possible people	Start date
Technical or functional tasks.		
Routine or repetitive tasks/ minor decisions.		
Projects offering development opportunities.		
Work offering more variety, job satisfaction or useful experience.		

4. The Better Meetings Campaign

The verdict on meetings

Long, long ago in the mid 1970s, when Ricky Gervais was but a lad and The Office not even dreamt of, it was John Cleese who struck lots of bells with corporate Britain and beyond with the best-selling Video Arts film, *Meetings, Bloody Meetings*. Followed closely with *More Bloody Meetings* on the art of chairmanship, the films depicted the daily disasters familiar to anyone who attended meetings. Some thirty years on, have things improved? Well not according to these recent surveys:

2001 – **Genesys Conferencing survey of senior management in 100 companies:**
- Communication is vital but meetings are a universal pain.
- 35% of directors and departmental managers said many of their meetings were unnecessary.
- One in four felt that 25-50% of time in important meetings was wasted.

2002 – **MORI poll for National Meetings Week:**
- 38% of meeting attendees think that too little of what is agreed at meetings then happens.
- 35% consider the meetings they attend to be generally dull, boring and a waste of time and money.
- 31% believe meetings are held out of habit and have no real purpose.

2003 – **ACT Teleconferencing:**
- The majority of people are switched off in meetings by a mixture of pointless updates, rambling speakers, meeting hijackers, bad visual aids and no refreshments.
- Managers and staff are using increasingly creative ways of evading meetings.
- 80% of meeting planners believe evasion is on the increase.

2003 – **The Mindmanager Effectiveness Survey Report:**
- Managers are spending too much time in meetings rather than managing.
- Meetings have become a noose round (managers') necks, preventing them from achieving their potential.

All the above survey findings paint a frightening picture of inefficiency. If we ran our factories like our meetings, our costs would be sky-high and we would be out of business.

So why not build support amongst colleagues for a "Better Meetings Campaign"? Taken from a variety of sources of best practice, and echoing the feedback from course participants over many years, I offer the following guidelines for you to develop…

> If we ran our factories like our meetings, our costs would be sky-high and we would be out of business.

Meeting Guidelines

1. Is the purpose TIMES?	6. Prepare and follow up.
2. Start and finish on time.	7. Listen and contribute.
3. Send agendas/timings/ reports in advance.	8. No interruptions, but do have breaks.
4. Review attendees.	9. Summarise.
5. Stay on track.	10. Send minutes promptly.

Figure 19

Meeting Guidelines

1. Is the purpose TIMES?

Why are you holding the meeting? Is it really necessary or should it be cancelled? Assuming it is necessary, the purpose usually fits under one of the following five headings (or some combination of them):

- **Training** – a meeting might be purely training or include a training element.
- **Informing** – staff or colleagues are updated about what is going on.
- **Motivating** – the purpose is to "rally the troops".
- **Endorsing** – appointments or reports might need endorsing or amending after suitable discussions.
- **Solving** – many meetings include elements of problem solving and decision making, a subject discussed in Session Four and discussed later in this section in relation to team development stages and meetings cultures.

2. Start and finish on time

What time does a two o'clock meeting start in your organisation? In one company I worked in my trainer gave me a tip. A two o'clock meeting meant being there at five minutes to two, so that you were sat down, papers sorted, and ready to start at two o'clock prompt.

In other organisations there is a culture that says, 'Our meetings never start on time, so there is no point being there for two o'clock.' As a result people drift in at various times, often missing the initial discussions, and are either unable to contribute fully or waste everybody's time with a recap.

You may even know some people who make a point of being late, either to demonstrate their power and authority or to show how busy and indispensable they are. Others are consistently late due to procrastination or sheer thoughtlessness. Creating a culture of starting a meeting on time, irrespective of who is or is not there, can start to save some of that wasted time mentioned in the surveys.

What about finish times? Centrally booked meetings of scarce meeting room space or on Microsoft Outlook or Lotus Notes have helped in many organisations by requiring a stated finish time. Yet too many organisations still do not have one. How on earth can you plan and schedule your time effectively if you do not know how long a meeting will last? Setting a target finish time tends to focus minds and discussions, whilst still allowing enough time for proper debate. For added flexibility, it is good practice to try and finish early, but have a maximum agreed overrun time of, say, half an hour, in the event of some vital issue warranting it. Anything unresolved at the end of this "extra time" is usually best left to another day.

> What time does a two o'clock meeting start in your organisation?

3. Send agendas, timings and reports in advance

Having no agendas or not getting an agenda until you arrive at the meeting is all too common. It makes a statement that the meeting is not worth preparing for (in which case, do you really need to hold the meeting?). Is there a clear purpose? Are there desired outcomes? Or is it a case of 'It's Tuesday and we always have a meeting on Tuesdays'?

Assuming you do need the meeting, some degree of time guideline on an agenda is helpful to ensure you spend the most time on the most important topics. And putting initials against the topic will clarify who is introducing it. You need to make sure each agenda item is clear. Simply putting "Communications" could mean that you want to introduce team briefings, a staff magazine, a new telephone exchange, or that you want to improve communication between departments. Spell it out. Make sure everyone comes prepared for the same discussion.

Finally on agendas, we need a word on Any Other Business, AOB. I am sure we have all seen this item needlessly prolong meetings or turn a positive one into a nit-picking negative one. Useful tactics to try or combine are:

- Have it at the beginning of the meeting to help you end on a high note.
- Strictly limit the time slot for AOB. If something needs a longer discussion, save it for the next meeting.
- Sift out items that are only of interest to a minority of people and cover them outside the meeting.
- Forbid AOB altogether, except in dire emergency.

Circulating reports in advance with the agenda is a real time saver. Too often, there is the "Ceremony of the Tree-Exchange", where people bring their reports to the meeting and pass them round, which takes time. Then, because colleagues have not had the chance to read them in advance, they present them, which takes even more time. But when people can read reports in advance of a meeting, they can pick out just the bits they want clarified or aired, thus saving time and raising the quality and value of the discussions.

4. Review attendees

The fewer the better for most meetings. Four to seven people are a good number for discussions and decisions. Appointing such a number as a "task force" or "action group" to tackle specific issues or projects can be very effective. Once you get over about a dozen attendees, participation and control become much more difficult.

To save everyone's time and improve meeting quality, try to keep the numbers down without upsetting people. Even when "the pecking order" says certain people should be there, they may be happy to be given the choice of not attending. Alternatively, having individuals or groups along for just parts of a meeting, to cover their special interest, is a simple and effective way of improving productivity.

5. Stay on track

Where interruptions are the rule, not the exception, meetings will take longer. What is your policy on mobile phones in meetings? On interruptions by colleagues and customers? Do you have re-energising, scheduled brain and comfort breaks in longer meetings (every one to two hours) or disruptive, unscheduled ones? How do you deal with each other when you wander off the point?

If your present arrangements are dysfunctional, change them! Agree what are allowable interruptions and what are not. Agree a "phones in meetings" policy. For wanderers off the point, bring them back on track with gentle reminders from colleagues or the chair about the topic under discussion.

6. Prepare and follow up

If you regularly find that you do not have time to prepare for meetings, make time! Block a slot in your diary to prevent it from being squeezed out by other things. Similarly, block some time in your diary for after a meeting. Most of us pick up some follow-up actions. Block in some time for this to ensure that what you are assigned to do you have time to do. This is especially important given the comments earlier in this section about too little of what is agreed at meetings actually happens.

7. Listen and contribute

Good meetings are about listening as well as talking. You can greatly increase your own chance of being heard and listened to by others if you can show that you have been actively listening to them. Do this by summarising what they have said in your own words before putting forward your own views. Those chairing meetings can increase listening by insisting on one conversation at a time. A simple "one meeting please" is usually sufficient to stop the distracting meetings-within-a-meeting.

On contributions to a meeting, we need to acknowledge that some people by their nature and preferred learning styles will always say more than others. Effective chairing of a meeting should ensure that the naturally reflective are invited to contribute and that the naturally verbose do not over-dominate.

Finally, to improve your own personal contribution to meetings, try putting ideas forward as suggestions rather than proposals. There is compelling evidence that if you do this, you are twice as likely to get support and half as likely to get difficulties stated. So 'What do you think about our doing a survey?' will usually get a better response than, 'I propose we do a survey.' This is strange but true. Try it.

8. Consider physical factors
It is all too easy to forget the basics. Are there enough chairs? Can people see the screen? Are there some flip chart pens? Is the place tidy? How is the temperature? Can distractions be minimised? Are drinks available? Of course, if you do not want your meeting to last long, you can always have no chairs and just stand up! This method is adopted by several organisations for, for instance, daily briefings or short group meetings on a single topic. The lack of seats certainly tends to focus the mind!

9. Summarise agreements
There are few experiences more frustrating than sitting in a meeting trying to agree on what you agreed at the previous meeting. Yet it still happens. The best way to overcome this is to have someone take down the action points and read them back to the meeting. This can be either as you go or in a summary session at the end. The alternative is to rely on the memory and skill of the minute-taker and/or chairperson, who may or may not agree with the recollection of others.

10. Send minutes promptly
Unless you have to have formal minutes for legal purposes, I would encourage the taking of brief, bulleted action points. These simply summarise what was agreed. They do not go into who said what. However, sometimes you may want to give a brief rationale for a decision if it will benefit non-attending recipients of the minutes. For a simple, easy-to-read format, action points should be in tabular, three-column format (a wide WHAT was agreed column, with a smaller WHO is accountable, and a similar sized by WHEN column). In most business meetings, these action points should be circulated quickly, say within 48 hours.

Team development stages

Most meetings are meetings of teams, whether of a department, project or task-focused team. And teams go through four well-documented stages in their development. Where they are in that cycle can affect not only their relationships with each other, but also their ability and readiness to make sound decisions, uncluttered by hidden agendas. The four stages are:

Forming – the initial awareness of why they are meeting both at the start of a new group and as new members join an existing one.
Storming – the sorting out process, with some muscle-flexing as people jockey for control and power.

Norming – a move from competition to collaboration and an improvement in the way they organise themselves and conduct the meetings.

Performing – where there is maturity and mutual acceptance, high loyalty and performance.

Can you detect which stage of development each of the meetings you attend is in? Is it affecting your ability to make sound decisions? If you want to learn about the subject of teams, books by Meredith Belbin and Edgar Schein are listed in the bibliography and can be found on the Amazon web site (www.amazon.co.uk).

Decision making at meetings

Listen to people coming out of meetings. Do you ever hear comments like, 'How on earth did we decide to do that?' 'Well I don't agree with it either.' 'Well it won't happen if I can help it.' With some meetings, such sounds of discontent are not uncommon. They reflect an unsatisfactory way of arriving at decisions. They result in a lack of commitment by some people to the decisions taken. And in turn, this can cause active or passive obstruction to implementing what was decided.

Adapted from the work of Edgar Schein, there are six different ways of making decisions. Each of them can be appropriate at different times, but to maximise commitment to decisions, it is useful to be conscious of the differences, rather than let them happen by accident. The six ways are:

Deaf ears
Someone suggests an idea, and before it is discussed, someone else suggests a different one. This can happen several times in a discussion before one suggestion is seized on, debated and agreed. The previous ideas appear to have fallen on deaf ears. Whilst sometimes this can be the kindest thing to happen to them, at other times, an alert chair or meeting member may need to rescue a potentially good idea before it is ignored and left unheard.

Chair power
One meeting chairman I knew ran very effective meetings in which he made all the key decisions. His method was to listen to everyone's views on a subject and make his decision when he had heard enough. He was effective because he happened to be a great listener and because he always ensured everyone had their say. So whilst his chair power ruled supreme, he had people's respect, won their commitment, and got through business at a very brisk pace. But without good listening skills, it is easy for this authoritarian method to backfire. People can feel uninvolved and not motivated to carry a decision through.

Minority rule
Silence is often taken as agreement. A proposal can be supported by one or two people. The chair asks, 'So, we're all agreed then?' People hesitate, perhaps thinking

they are the only discordant voice, and the lack of response is taken as support and the decision made. This is an excellent way of producing aggrieved meeting members. So beware of taking silence for agreement.

Majority rule

'Let's take a vote on it. Those in favour? Six. Against? Four. Motion carried!' This can be fine provided people feel they have had a fair opportunity to state their view. Often, however, the "losers" can spend their energies working out how to overturn the decision rather than implement it.

Consensus

This is different to the following unanimity. By consensus we mean that individuals, whilst not agreeing with what is proposed, nonetheless feel that they have had the chance to make their case. As such, they feel able to go along and support what the majority of their colleagues prefer to do. This is an excellent way of getting commitment, but does need more time than is sometimes available.

Unanimity

This may only really be necessary for some very key decisions, when it is absolutely crucial that everyone is of the same mind. Normally, however, achieving unanimity on every issue is a luxury few organisations can afford. Indeed, if everyone sees exactly the same way on every issue, beware of "Groupthink". Differing opinions usually create better outcomes than those from a Groupthink culture of cloned minds.

In general then, the more say people have in reaching decisions, the more committed they are to carrying them out. However, it also takes longer, and sometimes there is insufficient time to allow as full a debate on something as may be ideal, and the meeting's chair may have to decide.

Equally, there are some emotive topics such as the choice of company cars or organisational or salary issues, where input from the meeting can be invited and taken into account, but the final decision may still have to be taken by one individual. But, for commitment, the less this happens the better.

Meetings Charter

Summarising the ideas expressed above, here is a draft Meetings Charter for you to discuss within your organisation. You may copy it for this purpose. Why not debate it, amend it, agree it and follow it. Both you and your colleagues will then be in grave danger of saving a lot of time at meetings!

In our meetings we commit to…

1. **Starting on time** to respect the value of each other's time.
2. **Setting a realistic finish time** to help personal planning and scheduling.

3. **Circulating agendas and reports** before the meeting to ensure that the meeting is needed and to save time in the meeting by helping us be prepared.
4. **Having time guidelines and accountabilities** for agenda items, so that we spend more time on the more important issues.
5. **Reviewing who needs to attend** for the whole or just part of the meeting to reduce meeting costs and wasted time.
6. **Listening to each other** by having one conversation at a time and an open, constructive climate.
7. **Contributing to discussions** by not talking too much or too little and not wandering off the point.
8. **Scheduling personal time before and after a meeting** for preparation and follow-up action.
9. **Ensuring a good environment** with no interruptions and regular comfort breaks in longer meetings.
10. **Summarising what is agreed** and confirming this with succinct, prompt minutes or action points of who will do what and by when.

One-to-one meetings

They happen all the time. Whenever someone drops in to see you about something, it can easily escalate into a much longer session than planned, with little focus and unclear outcomes. To help these situations many people have found my PAT SAT acronym of Figure 20 useful.

One-to-one meetings

P urpose	Why are we meeting?
A genda	What must we cover?
T ime	What are our constraints?
S ummary	Check understandings.
A ction	Who will do what by when?
T ell	Who needs to know?

Figure 20

Train yourself at the start of all those ad hoc encounters to start it off PAT. 'Why are we meeting, what do we need to cover, and how long have we got?' Even this brief start might reveal that, to have a sensible discussion, you need Jill to be there and she is away until next week. So postpone the session until then. Getting an agreed agenda at the outset gives focus, and agreeing time constraints enables you to say by when you must be finished.

After your discussion use SAT. First of all summarise to ensure you both have a common understanding. Secondly, agree action points of who will do what by when, as you would in a normal meeting. And thirdly, decide who you need to tell about the outcome of your discussion. Informal the meeting may be. Unstructured it should not be. And productive it can be with PAT SAT.

Telephone, video and web conferencing

With increasing corporate concern about the unreliability of public transport, congested roads, security alerts, pressure on travel budgets, and the multi-siting of many national and international enterprises, more organisations are looking to technology for answers. Hence there is a growing interest in telephone, video and web-linked conferences.

We all know the value of telephone conversations and can therefore appreciate the added value of several people "meeting" on the phone. Add the visual dimension and the potential for PowerPoint presentations, web pages, spreadsheets and other shared documents, as well as "seeing" colleagues and customers, and the value of the new technology becomes evident. In addition, some formats allow more interactivity than the average meeting by means of "emotion" buttons. These allow participants to communicate their feelings to the chairperson throughout the conference. Some provide instant polling of whether people agree with the last point expressed or an overall presentation.

Electronic meetings seem destined to become increasingly commonplace and can be real time savers in certain situations. Business consultant Kevin Hardern, who has many years experience in implementing major projects as IT Programmes Director in Lloyds TSB, explains. 'We found telephone and video conferencing to be very useful for specific types of meeting such as crisis management, project implementation and progress reviews of delegated tasks' says Hardern. 'In fact, on some projects we could not have done without them, unless we had a different, less acceptable plan. In particular, telephone conferencing has been invaluable in getting key technicians and senior management "logically" together for "go/no go" decisions on major implementations.'

The UK Environment Agency is another great advocate of the new technology. With 120 video communication units across England and Wales, it believes it saved an annual £1.7million in costs, 1.5 million car miles, over half a million train miles, and an amazing 22 years of working days normally wasted through travel! It also improved morale by reducing the sense of isolation in some of their more remote sites.

Whilst the technology of these meetings is different, the basics of good preparation, good chairmanship, and the active involvement of all participants remain. In addition, there is the need to ensure before the meeting begins that the technology works and is properly set up. For video and web conferencing this includes capturing eye contact and body language, since over half our "message" is expressed in this way. Hardern also stresses the need for all participants to be literate in the technology protocols. Fortunately most electronic conferencing providers can give the necessary training.

The growing availability of broadband and its faster Internet connection can only accelerate the uptake of these new meeting methods, offering increased efficiency, reduced costs and saved time.

Meetings then, be they real or virtual, are a vitally important means of communication. They are here to stay. Yet the potential for improvement and time saving in many organisations is immense. Is yours one of them? If so, what are you going to do about it? Can you improve the meetings you attend or run? Can you influence meetings more widely? How about drawing up a brief action plan of what to do next?

Meetings Action Plan

Action	By whom	By when

5. Communicate! Communicate!

Surveys over the last ten years have regularly identified poor internal communications up, down and across organisations as a major time waster. We are back to our Session Two complaint about the lack of clairvoyants! The message is clear. If you are not to waste a lot of your time, you need to communicate clearly, and check understanding with key colleagues in other departments. If they understand what you are doing and why you are doing it, they are more likely to co-operate.

This is a classic "important-but-not-urgent" B activity, as discussed in Session Three. It can so easily get squeezed out of your plans. And it can so easily cause you grief from your colleagues. Four common causes of poor communications are crisis management, changing priorities, telephone skills and the inability to listen.

Crisis management

The time cultures in two branches of the same organisation were totally different. One branch was constantly getting into customer service scrapes and then rescuing itself by rushing around, pulling out all the stops, and using up lots of macho nervous energy in the process.

A sister branch, on the other hand, had an air of quiet competence about it. Whenever it got into a scrape, it also did a rescue job, but then analysed what had gone wrong and set about preventing it from happening again.

The first branch was a "crisis junkie"! Everyone got sucked into the frenetic pace and the "get it right second time" mentality. The culture was set by the top managers. They thrived on the thrill and adrenaline of sorting out the crisis of the day. Unfortunately, they made people under them crisis junkies too. So these top managers were also crisis pushers! And such crisis pushers can be seen alive and well in many organisations.

The effect is very often to drive away good people who get frustrated with the lack of sound organisational planning and a constant "red alert" reactive way of working. It is easy to get left with a core of like-minded "all action, no planning" group whose shelf-life in today's increasingly competitive and demanding market place has got to be questioned.

Changing priorities

It can be frustrating to work on a report or to provide some information requested by colleagues, only to find that when you produce it it is not needed. 'Oh sorry, things changed,' they say. 'We've moved on since then'. All well and good, but it would of have been nice to have been told! Remember that **'To err is human, but when the eraser runs out ahead of the pencil, you're overdoing it.'** J. Jenkins

So with persistent changed priorities, is it evidence of colleagues being "full-steam adrift", lacking clear goals and direction as outlined in Session Two? Or, is it a dose of crisis management, perhaps centred around one or more "crisis junkies" mentioned above? Whatever the cause, for repeat offenders, try and arrange a "managing the boundaries communication exercise".

Managing The Boundaries Exercise

List below the departments that have the greatest interface with yours.

Where communications or co-operation is suspect, either set up a meeting with each of these departments in turn or suggest this to your manager. You could use the following agenda:

1. What are the main ways they affect your time?
2. What are the main ways you affect their time?
3. What is the cost to the company of this?
4. What can both of you do differently that might improve understanding and save time?
5. What will be done by whom, and by when, to make this happen?
6. How will you monitor this?
7. When will you review progress?

Telephone skills

In Session Four we spoke of voicemail as an aid to reducing interruptions during our Red Time. Here are some more time-saving telephone tips…

By doing calls in blocks, rather than as they occur, you will be in "telephone mode", and find you get through them quicker and with less disruption to your day. Set aside space in your organiser to jot down the purpose of your call and bullet points of what you want to cover. Similarly, during the call, remember that a short pencil is better than a long memory, so take notes. And to reduce the "telephone tag" game, consider whether someone else may be able to help you if the person you are ringing is not there.

If you know anyone whose calls tend to be long-winded, suggest they try using an egg timer as a fun way to monitor their calls. It is often possible to use the "nicely direct" approach we mentioned for office interruptions. Discuss the business, summarise the outcome, and have a friendly farewell, all within the time it takes to soft-boil an egg! This is made easier if you can phone near to lunch time or towards the end of the day.

Research shows that the number one requirement for good customer service is reliability. So a must for telephone usage is to be reliable in keeping your promises to both your external and internal customers alike. Whether these are messages on your voicemail that you will contact people by the end of the day, or promises you make during a call, build up a reputation for doing what you say you will do.

> By doing calls in blocks, rather than as they occur, you will be in "telephone mode", and find you get through them quicker and with less disruption to your day.

Inability to listen

'If only they had listened!' 'No-one ever listens around here.' 'You are not listening to me.' How many times have we heard these phrases? Surely, if ever there was an under-rated skill it is listening. Some people think listening means stopping talking, whilst they think about what to say next. Some people hear, but do not listen.

> **I know you believe you understand what you think I said, but I am not sure you realise that what you heard is not what I meant.** Anon.

Common barriers to good listening are physical barriers, fears, "solutionitis", "assumptionitis", concerns about the messenger obscuring the message, and preoccupation with our own thoughts.

Physical barriers
Noise, discomfort or distractions need to be identified and removed.

Fears
Some people are nervous about hearing things they might not want to hear, or being asked questions to which they do not know the answers. They therefore prefer to stay within their personal "comfort zone". Such people need to learn that without listening they will never understand. But once understanding is achieved, answers can be sought. It is no sign of weakness not to know all the answers. It is a sign of weakness not to listen to all the questions.

"Solutionitis"
This is a common complaint. Sufferers believe they know the solution before they have heard the full story and so interrupt. Often they are wrong. Even when they are right, the speaker can be left with the feeling that they were not really listening at all. The remedy is patience, learnt with practise and active listening (which I will cover shortly).

"Assumptionitis"
This is a similar condition. Sufferers engage in selective listening. They quickly assume they have heard this problem or been in this situation before. Their brain obligingly screens out any inconvenient facts which conflict with this view. Active listening will help them to question similarities and look for differences. This transforms "assuming" understanding into "confirming" understanding.

The messenger
Messengers can sometimes get in the way of their message.

> **What you are, speaks so loudly, that I cannot hear what you are saying.**
> Waldo Emerson.

We see this in ethnic conflicts, our own political parties, and even between colleagues or departments in some organisations. When trust or credibility dips below a certain level, it can easily become a case of whatever the other party does or says is wrong. This not only impairs the ability to listen, it tends to produce lose/lose outcomes. In such cases, an impartial mediator may be needed if one side is ever to really listen to the other.

Preoccupation with our own thoughts
This can sometimes impair our listening. The problem, but also the solution, lies in the speed at which we listen and talk. It seems that we can listen at three to four times the speed at which people normally talk. With this unused spare capacity, the brain can quickly go off on a journey of its own. It returns part-way through a conversation, wondering what has been said and what has been missed. Everyone, I suspect, is familiar with this.

Active listening

One way of overcoming these barriers is active listening. As shown in Figure 21, this involves listening with your ears, eyes and feet.

Listening with ears, eyes and feet

- ■ **EARS** for key points, assumptions, facts and opinions.
- ■ **EYES** for body language, emotions and feelings.
- ■ **FEET** for putting yourself in their shoes.

- ■ **REFLECT** back in your own words:

  - ▪ What they feel.
  - ▪ About what.
  - ▪ And why.

Figure 21

Use your ears, as well as the aforementioned spare capacity in the brain, to listen for what is actually being said beneath the words. What are the key points? Where is the argument going? Are there any implied assumptions? Are you hearing facts or opinions? Meanwhile, the eyes are taking in the body language of the speaker. Are they calm, agitated, angry, happy or what?

And then listen with your feet. Can you put yourself in the speaker's shoes? Can you understand where the person is coming from? How might you feel in a similar situation?

Having actively listened to the other person, reflect back to them in your own words what they have said. Express it to them in their terms as to what they feel, about what and why. For instance, 'So as I understand it, you feel angry and disappointed that nobody discussed these changes with you, even though it is your department that is mainly affected?'

The benefit of this is that you either demonstrate that you have been listening and understand their point of view, or give them the opportunity to correct anything you got wrong. Furthermore, you have done this without at this stage saying whether you agree with them or not. You have also earned a better hearing for any contrary view you may have. If you follow this route, no one can say that 'you do not understand', because you have just demonstrated that you do. It is an invaluable skill, which you can practise on friends and colleagues in many situations.

In summary, actively listening with your ears, eyes and feet, wins you respect and saves you time.

6. Ensuring time management training is not a waste of time

With all the problems of managing time felt by workforces worldwide, the importance of time management training might seem self-evident. Yet several writers believe that earlier forms of time management training simply do not work. Further, in a recent review of the literature, only one study found that it did work, whilst five found no such evidence!

However, in 2002, a study of 19 courses based on the contents of the first edition of this book, all produced measurable improvements in personal effectiveness some months after the course. This was based on the self-reported scores of 134 participants, against the key time management skills covered in the book and listed on pages 161 and 162. Participants' managers, who agreed or tended to agree with 95% of the scores, confirmed the findings. Only 5% tended to disagree – split equally between concerns of over and under-scoring. Furthermore, these managers were able to describe qualitative evidence of improvement. The research, conducted through Oxford Brookes Business School, is now the subject of an academic article.

An example of the "added value" from one of the training courses (a police force IT team – approved by them for publication) is shown in Figure 22.

Whilst the average improvement was 20%, there were wide personal variations from +141% to -10%, as shown in Figure 23. This is consistent with research on non-training factors that affect training outcomes. These are listed in the "unblock your learning" section in Session One. From all this, conclusions can be drawn to help increase your organisation's Return On Training (ROT).

Training value added

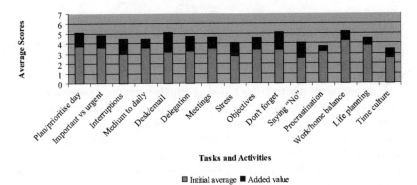

Figure 22

More ROT (Return On Training)

To maximise the return on the time management training pound, there is a need to train early, train modern, be supportive and follow up.

1. Train early
The research described in the last section showed that the average improvement in personal effectiveness was 20%. This figure matches the 20% time wasted reported in a 1993 Industrial Society survey. The inference is that in many organisations, considerable numbers of management, professional and sales staff are operating at well below their optimum level. The sooner such people can be trained in effective time management practices, the sooner their employers will benefit from increased effectiveness. Delaying the training prolongs the inefficiency, lowers productivity, creates stress and increases absenteeism.

There is, therefore, a strong case to be made for time management training to be included in induction training programmes.

Individual improvements

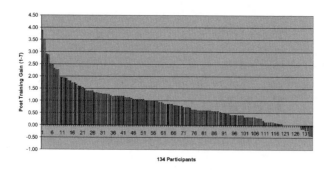

134 Participants

Figure 23

2. Train modern

However, that training needs to be based on modern time management content. Stephen Covey and colleagues usefully categorise four generations of time management. The first generation is based on reminders and is characterised by simple notes and checklists. The second generation adds more planning, preparation, goal setting and scheduling, featuring calendars and appointments on paper or computer. The third generation adds prioritising and control, with a review of values, the setting of long to short-term goals, and daily prioritising, often in electronic or paper-based organisers.

Covey believes that these earlier approaches to time management simply do not work. They fail to allow people to match what they consider to be important with how they actually spend their time. Noon expresses similar sentiments, believing that we cannot keep doing more work in less time just because the work is there to be done.

A fourth generation of time management is, therefore, advocated by Covey. This includes the best features of earlier generations, but focuses on identifying what is really important in life, and spending an increasing amount of time on that. In a similar vein, Noon advocates what he terms a "reductionist" stance, which involves eliminating all unnecessary work, learning to say "no" and, like Covey, focusing on what is important.

This book agrees with and reflects these views. If the proof of the pudding is in the eating, then the research on the 19 courses based on this book shows that this approach does work. So, as many earlier methods did not, ensure you train modern.

3. Be supportive

Training evaluation guru Donald Kirkpatrick has a five-point scale to measure management support. This ranges from "preventing" people from implementing training ideas and discouraging them at one extreme, through neutral, to encouraging and positively expecting people to use new ideas learnt at the other. Two people in this latter category were the two managers involved in the police IT course mentioned in Figure 22. During the training itself they made on-the-spot agreements with their teams to implement various ideas as they arose. It is, therefore, not surprising that with an average 20% improvement from the course, their course showed a 36% gain.

So supportive management can have a big influence on post-training performance. Involving people in the identification of, and solution to, their training needs also helps, as well as encouragement, showing interest in what was learnt and applied, seeking sufficient resources to do the job, and opportunity to practise the new skills.

4. Follow up

This is also very important. For instance, in the research project, whilst 89% of people showed a positive improvement, 7% recorded no change, and 4% recorded worse scores! Following up on the latter categories, it was possible to identify some underlying, often non-training problems. Coaching and counselling in some of these cases was then able to remove some of the barriers to applying the learning, thereby further improving the Return On Training.

In summary, whilst earlier research had suggested that time management training was a waste of money, new research contradicts this view. Instead, it is the failure to train and support people properly in this vital work and life skill that is – literally – a waste of time.

SUMMARY OF SESSION FIVE: People Time

1. Develop a professional working relationship with your boss, mindful that you will always have three options if you are unhappy with this.
2. Good bosses get results from their people by directing, developing and motivating them by AGREEMENT.
3. Multiply your time by improving your delegation skills when you give and receive delegated tasks using the TIARA acronym.
4. Suggest a Meetings Charter to save time, improve their quality, and increase commitment to decisions made at them.
5. Improve communications by "managing the boundaries" with other parts of the organisation to reduce the dangers of crisis management and constantly changed priorities.
6. Maximise the return on your time management training by training early, training modern, being supportive and following up.

Session

6

Session Six: Paperwork And The Modern Office

The paperless office is a myth. Indeed, there is **more** paper used nowadays, not less. So we still have paper to manage as well as electronic mail (email) and other Information Technology (IT) to keep up-to-date with and master. Therefore, in this Session we cover:

1. Your time toolkit choices.
2. How to manage paper.
3. Paper file management.
4. Email – profit or cost centre?
5. Managing your Inbox.
6. Managing your Outbox.
7. Faster report writing.

1. Your time toolkit choices

It is no good knowing how to manage your time if you do not have the tools to implement the theory. Which set of tools you use (paper-based, electronic, or a combination) is much less important than the fact that you do use something. And sorry, those scraps of paper, post-its, various notepads (not to mention backs of envelopes) do not constitute a time system – unless you like stress of course, in which case they are ideal!

Stress reduction is one of the tangible benefits offered by a decent time system. Knowing that all your thoughts and messages are contained in one place and that consequently the risk of forgetting things or failing to follow up is reduced can only serve to increase peace of mind.

Your time toolkit options nowadays are extensive. On electronic versions, you can go desktop, laptop or palm-top. On paper-based versions you can go from credit card wallet size up to A4 size, with A5 being the most popular.

> It is no good knowing how to manage your time if you do not have the tools to implement the theory.

In theory, you would think that paper systems had had their day and that electronics would rule the world. For instance, most business people use email, many arrange their appointments on a company Intranet computer system, and customer records can be much more detailed and easily shared as electronic, rather than paper files. Also palm-top Personal Data Assistants (PDAs) can allow out-of-office travellers to stay connected with access to email, corporate data, telephone and web-based information.

But as a 2002 Filofax "Power of Paper" survey of 1,000 senior managers revealed, more than half of them found it quicker and easier to write things down and track vital information on paper rather than electronically. Finding a page can sometimes be faster than finding a screen. Certainly I can plan and prioritise a "To Do" list (as discussed earlier in the book) much more quickly on paper than others can electronically. Four out of ten people interviewed in the survey had a fear of product failure and memory loss with electronic organisers. Furthermore, a finding of the time management research project mentioned earlier was that paper-based organisers do seem to offer a means of implementing the theory learnt from books and training, though more research is still needed on this.

Whilst there are some individuals at either end of the "no paper" and "only paper" spectrum, the situation in which most of us find ourselves is how best to blend the respective powers of paper and computer. One example is the selective use of printouts of key information, such as contact lists and computerised diary appointments kept in a paper-based organiser. Another is a PDA wallet including a small notepad.

> Both paper and electronic organisers are only a means to an end, not an end in themselves. The real end is the effective use of your time to achieve your work and life goals.

There are, however, common messages from across virtually all the time management literature. The first is that it is a matter of personal preference, probably involving some trial and error. The second is that both paper and electronic organisers are only a means to an end, not an end in themselves. The real end is the effective use of your time to achieve your work and life goals.

In summary, I recommend that you use what you feel most comfortable with, provided it works and produces results for you. Staying with the paper and electronic debate, we now look at how to manage paper mail and electronic mail.

2. How to manage paper

Desk management

Imagine you are on the telephone and I come up to your desk and say, 'Carry on with your telephone conversation whilst I tell you about your new job in Inverness. Of course you will have to move up there and the pay is slightly less. But then you won't have any staff to worry about and I believe it is cheaper living up there and…Why have you stopped talking on the phone?'

Is it fair to say that very few if any of us are capable of carrying on two conversations of that nature at the same time? There is a simple explanation. Our conscious brain, brilliant though it is, is only capable of concentrating on one thing at a time.

You know this. How many times in the past have you sat at your desk, working on say a report, when: 'Oh look! There is the last sales report. How did we do last week? No, no! I must do the report. Although... Is that that article I meant to read? It looks very interesting. Sorry! The report. Yes. Ah! That's where my expense report got to. Now how much was it for?'

We are all so easily distracted, especially when we are doing a difficult task or one where we need to stop and think. We need to give our brains a chance. Yet a "Clear Your Desk" survey of 1,000 managers and executives across various industries found that 93% of them worked with a cluttered desk. Each piece of paper on it distracted people up to five times a day, and they spent about 35 minutes each day simply looking for misplaced documents. This becomes 45 minutes each day if you include the filing system!

Remove the distractions! Clear the desk! One piece of paper on your desk at a time might be extreme and impractical. But one subject on your desk at a time is not extreme and is very practical. So scoop up all those piles of papers or piles of files. Put them in one neat pile, wearing a safety helmet if the height is dangerous! Polish the desk as you clear any other debris away and feel the stress roll away as we now look at paper management.

Paper management

Watching people return from holiday and cope with the paper mountain in their in-tray can be quite entertaining. Three common approaches are:

- **The Paper Shufflers** who shuffle everything into various piles on their desk, often scooping them all up again at the end of the day and repeating the process the next day.
- **The Jugglers** who try to work on several papers together, picking one up, putting it down, picking another up, putting it down, and never quite finishing anything.
- **The Top Downers** who start at the top of the pile and work their way down before the next lot of papers goes on top and they never do find out what is at the bottom of the pile.

Paper management kit

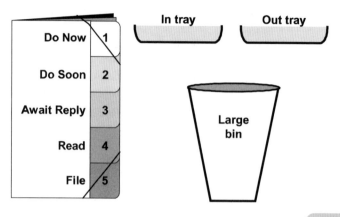

Figure 24

None of these methods is productive and all can create stress. The answer for most of us lies in the simple paper management kit shown in Figure 24. Course participants have so far failed to come up with any paper hitting their desk which could not come under one of the five headings or go in either the bin or the out tray.

This system will enable you to skim through a huge pile of mail in a very short time. You can get to the bottom of the in tray and know that all the important items that need action are now in the "Do Now" section of the five-part expanding file or paperwork organiser. The latter are easily available in five, seven, nine and twelve- part formats from any stationers or you may well have some in your organisation's stationery store.

Having skimmed through the mail, you then tackle the "Do Now" papers in order of priority, using the same rationale as you use for planning the day. The "Do Soons" may include some important but not urgent B's. Equally, they may include items that seemed like a good idea at the time you put them there, but which on reflection, may now be seen to be less important than first thought. These can be safely disregarded and discarded.

The "Await Reply" section is useful as a home to keep and help monitor returns of information or responses from other people. An alternative to this is a "Tickler" or "Bring Forward File". This is a 1-31 section concertina file. If you have asked for responses by the 14th, you put your memo in section 14, and by checking the appropriate section each day your memory is "tickled" to send out any reminders that might be needed.

Especially when your desk starts to look messy, I strongly recommend the use of this paper management system to clear it. You will also reduce the feeling of being overwhelmed with paper and feel more in control by knowing what papers you have and where they are. Whilst the method does not meet the ideal criteria of "handling each piece of paper only once", it comes close. You only handle each item twice, one of these being the initial quick sort.

Reading management

After "Await Reply" comes the reading section. And on reading, I recommend that you learn to skim through your magazines and publications very fast, looking for items of interest. If your job requires you to do a lot of reading, especially of technical material, you might consider investing in a book or possibly a course on speed reading. These offer proven techniques that can often double your reading speed whilst maintaining if not improving your comprehension.

It is interesting to note that on some Buzan speed reading courses (see the bibliography), participants find they only need to read two to ten per cent of their magazines' contents. On that basis, you only need to read a tiny fraction of each publication.

You might look at reducing the number of publications you receive and cutting out or photocopying for filing just the items of interest, before throwing the rest of the magazine into the recycling bin. Lest we overdo all this, however, remember the words of the late Isaac Foot:

Men of power have no time to read, yet men who do not read are unfit for power.

3. Paper file management

If at present you can file and retrieve documents easily, quickly and consistently, I suggest you do not change anything. If, however, you are less than happy with your filing, and spend the average person's time of 45 minutes each day looking for documents on the desk or in the filing system read on!

Here is a method of filing that I know works well. At one time I spent part of each week in an office in Dundee, and part of the week 400 miles away at home in Aylesbury. Using the system I am about to describe, I had my files written out on two sides of an A4 sheet and was able to access them by phone. If I can work a filing system from 400 miles away, might it have something to offer you? It is based on your key areas (you may already have decided what these are in Session One). To give you an idea of how it works, Figure 25 shows a possible system for a sales executive, based on the sales key areas listed on page 21.

1.0	COMPANY COMMUNICATIONS		6.0	PERFORMANCE PLANNING & CONTROL	

1.0 COMPANY COMMUNICATIONS
- **1.1 Company publications**
  - 1.1.1 Company history
  - 1.1.2 Annual reports
- **1.2 Sales publications**
  - 1.2.1 Sales bulletins
  - 1.2.2 Quarterly review
- **1.3 Team communications**
  - 1.3.1 Sales Manager
  - 1.3.2 Sales colleagues
  - 1.3.3 Sales office
  - 1.3.4 Other departments
2.0 CUSTOMERS (A-Z)
3.0 CALL PLANNING
- **3.1 Journey plans**
- **3.2 Weekly call plans**
4.0 PROSPECTS (A-Z)
5.0 PRODUCT & MARKETING INFORMATION
- **5.1 Price lists**
  - 5.1.1 Year-round lines
  - 5.1.2 Seasonal lines
  - 5.1.3 Promotional lines
- **5.2 Product information (A-Z)**
- **5.3 Competitor information (A-Z)**
- **5.4 Industry information**
  - 5.4.1 Trade magazines
  - 5.4.2 Press Cuttings (date order)

6.0 PERFORMANCE PLANNING & CONTROL
- **6.1 Sales targets**
- **6.2 Quarterly summary**
- **6.3 Target achievements**
- **6.4 Sales performance tables**
- **6.5 Sales objectives**
7.0 PERSONAL DEVELOPMENT
- **7.1 Performance appraisals**
- **7.2 Field visit appraisals**
- **7.3 Sales courses**
- **7.4 Sales meetings**
- **7.5 Product knowledge checklist**
- **7.6 Sales qualifications**

PERSONAL
- Family
- Friends
- Financial
- Hobbies & Interests
- Holidays
- House

IDEAS
Write them down as you think of them!

PROJECTS
Any major project in which you are involved, such as special committee, report on competitor etc.

Figure 25

With the combination of numbering and use of letters for, say, customers and products (2.0 and 5.2), this method gives a simple, understandable framework. It has worked for others. Could it work for you?

Clutter management

Whether or not you change your filing, you can help to find papers more easily by having regular clear-out sessions. An increasing number of companies now organise "Bin Bag Days" to do this. Everyone is given the familiar black bin liner and asked to clear out (and hopefully recycle) all the junk and out-of-date paper currently cluttering up their desk drawers and filing systems.

It can be embarrassing. Your less well-organised colleagues are in danger of finding many of the customer letters, memos, credit notes, urgent orders, or other items that they have been frantically looking for over the past few weeks and months. And that is just their desks!

The potential for the filing system is even greater when you consider that:

- 85% of what we file we never look at again.
- The average office worker in Europe generates 5,000 extra sheets of paper each year and only gets rid of 3,000.

- Professor George Bain of the London Business School is quoted as saying, 'I have an annual purge to restructure the (filing) system and I say, "What's essential? What shall we keep? Who else holds papers on this topic? Do we really need this?" I'm fairly ruthless about chucking stuff out.'
- Sir John Harvey-Jones says, 'My main filing aid is a waste paper basket.' (And remember that with your computer files, your waste paper basket is called the delete button!)

So, clear out the clutter, review and purge your filing system to help you find things more easily and with less stress. And now from paper management, we move to electronic management.

4. Email – profit or cost centre?

Email is both one of the greatest savers and wasters of our time. In this section we will look at the use and abuse which has led to its phenomenal growth, the potential costs to individuals and organisations, and the consequent need to manage In and Out boxes carefully.

Email growth

Email is now the most predominant method of communicating in business. According to International Data Corporation, 5 billion emails per day were sent in 1999. This doubled to 10 billion in 2000, rose to 15 billion by 2002, and is forecast to be 35 billion emails per day by 2005.

A variety of factors have contributed to this astonishing exponential growth. There has been an obvious switch from paper memos, faxes and voicemail messages to email as the preferred communications route. Many people have increased responsibilities, as discussed earlier in the book, and consequently need to communicate on more issues. Email volumes have also grown from various abuses of the medium and these will be considered shortly.

These abuses though should not detract us from the very real benefits email offers. At the click of a mouse, our thoughts can be fired off to multiple destinations on every continent, with an attached file of words, charts or pictures of almost any size if we so wish. Colleagues can simultaneously have input on a presentation, proposal or plan on their own screen and send it back to us in a flash, day or night. It enables us to communicate up, across and down an organisation with a speed and ease never afforded by paper. It is inexpensive to the sender and has offered a new way of marketing our goods and services to potential clients in many markets and languages. It even provides an audit trail. Email is wonderful. What a boon! What an invention!

Email abuses

However, if it's that good, why in 2003 did Phones4U boss John Caudwell follow the earlier example of Nestlé Rowntree and Liverpool City Council in banning the use of internal email? His action received international media coverage. He claimed that his people were spending three hours a day on email, and that the ban would save him a million pounds a month. A company spokesman told the Guardian, 'We want to get people using the most effective form of communication for the task.' One of the dangers is that it makes people lazy, so rather than thinking about who needs to be sent information people 'write a quick email and copy 20 people in'. So the abuses we shall look at now are misuse of the copy button, the wrong channel, attitude issues, and the volume of spam or junk emails.

1. Too many cc's

Professor Christina Cavanagh's research points to internal organisational factors as the main drivers in increased email volumes. The prime one of these is the increased use of the carbon copy (cc) button, pulling in a wider circle of people on an email topic. This habit of sending copies of memos to the world and his wife may be because of a lack of thought or a company culture of "cover my back".

Notwithstanding that, the ability to inform lots of people about something at the same time, at the click of a button, is often cited (especially by senior managers) as one of email's great strengths. Yet any strength when overdone becomes a weakness. Confidence is a strength, but when overdone becomes arrogance. Similarly, the ease of copying messages to people is a strength of email which, when overdone, becomes a weakness, contributing to information overload and attendant costs to individuals and organisations. Care is therefore needed as to whom, if anyone, really needs a copy of the emails we send.

2. Wrong channel

The ease of sending an email can also result in people taking that route even when it is not the most appropriate channel of communication. To avoid long "ping-pong" exchanges of emails, it is sometimes quicker and better to pick up the phone, have a face-to-face meeting, or write a letter. Bearing in mind that our messages are conveyed only 7% by words, 38% by our tone of voice, and 55% by our body language, it is obvious that face-to-face meetings can use all three senses, telephone calls the first two, and emails only the 7%.

> The ease of copying messages to people is a strength of email which, when overdone, becomes a weakness, contributing to information overload and attendant costs to individuals and organisations.

Opportunities for misunderstanding emails are therefore rife. This calls for more careful planning and writing than was originally envisaged in the early "honeymoon days" of the new medium. Cavanagh's book, *Managing Your E-Mail: Thinking Outside The Inbox*, gives the following guidelines on when to use email, telephone, face-to-face or written communications.

Email is best for formal communications for a specific purpose, for a distinct audience. It suits fact-based requests where non-verbal body language signals are not important. Complex emails may sometimes be best responded to by telephone or in person.

The telephone is best for specific, urgent situations, and for content-related issues, the fine-tuning of plans, and to reinforce and extend relationships.

Face-to-face meetings are best for developing relationships, for negotiating, generating ideas, solving problems, resolving conflicts, discussing workplace performance and making sales visits.

Written communications can be used to supplement information from other channels and to confer authority on, for instance, internal or external consultants' reports. Email is not a secure medium and can be intercepted at numerous points in its journey. Therefore, written communications are usually best for sensitive and confidential matters such as personnel issues, competitive information or research findings.

3. Attitude issues
Three common attitudes associated with email are:

Laziness
The ease of copying people in can lead to the laziness the Phones4U spokesman mentioned earlier. The problem is echoed in Cavanagh's research, where respondents noted the switch from the valuable MBWA to the lazier MBNWA (Management By Not Wandering Around). A common manifestation of this is persistently emailing a colleague two screens away when a simple face-to-face exchange might be a much better and quicker option.

Availability
Some people only seem to communicate by email at the expense of all other methods. Rather than make them more effective, it usually annoys colleagues and hinders rather than helps good relationships.

Expectations
You may know people who expect everyone to be sat by their computers just waiting for and instantly reacting to every email. They cannot understand why everyone did not immediately pick up the last minute change of a meeting time, place or agenda item they sent. They need to be educated that this is neither an effective use of time nor a reasonable expectation.

4. TUNA and spam

TUNA (Totally Uninteresting News and Admin) is a term coined by Dr John Gundry for internal junk email, brother of its better-known external version, spam. Examples of TUNA include when employees at all sites are emailed that 'the staff restaurant on one site will close early next Wednesday' or that 'the stationery store will be stocktaking on Tuesday'. Occasional TUNA is digestible. Regular TUNA is not.

As for spam, the Chartered Institute of Marketing (CIM) web site reports that:

- Microsoft blocks around 2.4 billion junk emails a day, some 80% of the messages that hit their network servers.
- BT Openworld estimates that 41% of the 25 million emails it monitors are spam.
- It is predicted that by 2006 there will be twenty billion daily spam messages sent worldwide.

Is it any wonder that the UK and other governments are introducing legislation to curb this excess? The 2003 Privacy and Electronic Communications Regulations Act requires UK marketers to have permission from consumers before sending marketing material via email. By 2010, the CIM predicts a move from a communications free-for-all to an age of consent. This will involve a shift from a model of intrusion to one of communicating and building relationships through collaboration. In the short term, despite corporate firewalls and filters that block out large amounts of unwanted traffic, spam will increase and will need to be managed.

Email volumes and costs

Cavanagh cites the average number of daily emails received by managers in a range of industries in Canada and America as 48 in 2002. In the same year, in the UK's Department for International Development (DFID), the average figure for senior managers was remarkably similar at 50. Within these averages there are of course wide variations, with some people receiving fewer than ten a day whilst others receive over a hundred.

What is manageable and what is not? Two markers can be put down here. 25 emails received per day is manageable. 100 emails received per day is not. The numbers in-between are contentious. Let me explain.

Cavanagh's research shows that 64%, or two out of three emails, require a response. Thus 25 emails per day, plus responses, gives a total of 41 emails. Respondents to Cavanagh's research and in-company work indicate that this is manageable. The DFID report supports this, finding that senior managers were comfortable with a daily in and out combined total of 20 to 50 emails.

However, the DFID report also concluded that 100 incoming emails per day was simply not manageable for senior civil servants, even with the active involvement of a senior secretary. If 4 hours were available for desk work in-between meetings, this leaves only 2.4 minutes available to deal with each email, including responses to two thirds of them! Clearly this is not feasible.

> People receiving the recorded average of 48 emails per day are receiving more information than they need, can read, or are able to manage without working longer hours.

Cavanagh concurs but goes further. In her experience, people receiving the recorded average of 48 emails per day are receiving more information than they need, can read, or are able to manage without working longer hours. In her view, at 25 messages per day, the benefits far outweigh the costs. At 40 or more per day, she believes the productivity costs become marginal. At 50 plus, they are costing both individuals and their organisations.

Supporting this belief is her annual email productivity study. This showed that over the last two years, where average emails received reached 48 per day, 70% of respondents were spending on average an extra one and a quarter hours per day in handling the increase. This is on top of the average two to two and a half hours they were spending two years ago. This time must either come from longer hours or having less time to work on the value-adding, important but not urgent "B" tasks. There is no evidence to suggest that this extra time is helping productivity, mission or profits.

As for your own productivity, how many emails **you** can cope with will depend on several factors. These include the nature of the email content, your speed of skimming and deleting unwanted mail, and the amount of thought and consideration typically needed for your responses. Before you decide on a final figure of what is comfortable for you, consider any hidden time costs, such as doing emails at home, at the weekend, or alas, as many people do, on holiday.

A further factor is your typing speed. Online typing courses might be helpful here. Alternatively, voice-to-screen software has made major strides forward in recent years. It is now possible to enjoy all the benefits of the keyboard with about 90 minutes training on software such as Dragon.

In summary, whilst everyone wanted to keep their email, the top dislike of it in Cavanagh's findings is that there is too much of it. Having looked at some of the underlying reasons for this, let us try and quantify the costs involved.

Quantifying the cost of excess email

Using various assumptions on how long things take, Cavanagh calculates the extra cost of handling 50 emails a day, rather than a reasonable 25, to be £3 million a year for a company with 1,000 employees. This would be £9 million for a 3,000 strong workforce such as Phones4U. You will recall they quoted a £1 million per month saving, or £12 million per year, a figure close to Cavanagh's and thereby adding further credence to her work. However, these figures do not include the hidden costs of stress that overwhelming workloads can bring.

Incidentally, like most commentators on the telephone company's action, rather than a ban, I would prefer to see increased awareness and training on effective email management of In and Outboxes.

5. Managing your Inbox

In the first edition of this book, I recounted the true story of the first day of a new chief executive. Faced with a mountain of mail on his desk, he threw it all in the bin. He reassured his incredulous PA that she would be surprised how few people got back to him about anything in those papers. He was proved right.

The electronic mail equivalent example is provided in Cavanagh's *Managing Your E-mail* book. She explains how the president of a multinational corporation was separated from his email for a few days and found 290 messages in the Inbox. Realising he could not possibly deal with them all he deleted the lot. As with the paper example, only a couple of people followed up seeking a response.

Disclaimer – attractive though this might sound, I am not recommending you do this yourself! The stories are told to illustrate the fact that sometimes the volume of mail facing us is simply unmanageable. In such cases, the above stories may embolden you to use the delete button more freely.

Deleting is one of the 20 tips on managing your Inbox (summarised in Figure 26) which we consider next.

1. **Guidelines**
   We all differ in our emails in terms of volumes, content, culture and job role. The following suggestions are, therefore, guidelines for you to adapt flexibly, rather than tablets of stone for you to follow slavishly.

2. **Checking**
   Mention was made in Session Four of the need to restrict the number of times per day you check your emails. Deactivating anything that tells you there is new mail reduces your distraction count. Checking and actioning your email in blocks of time rather than piecemeal will keep you more focused and shorten the time needed to go through them.

3. Software

The more emails you receive the more important it is to master your email software. You can benefit from using such features as filters, folders, files, preview pane, archiving and the out-of-office assistant. If you are unsure about any of these, try your personal computer guru, colleagues, software manuals, online help, training providers, or Learn Direct, who offer courses on software at libraries and other venues throughout the country. Many courses are free and can often be accessed via home or office computers. It is also a useful idea to set up a "How To" page in your organiser, where you jot down what you need to be able to do. When you find out from any of the above sources, jot down the key strokes involved to save time next time around.

20 Inbox tips

1. Guidelines	11. Printing
2. Checking	12. Reading
3. Software	13. Previewing
4. Filters	14. Prioritising
5. Folders	15. Actioning
6. CC Folders	16. Educating
7. Files	17. Clearing
8. Skimming	18. Archiving
9. Deleting	19. Influencing
10. Series	20. Accessing

Figure 26

4. Filters

Once you receive a piece of junk mail you can assign all future mail from that address to a junk mail bin without it reaching your Inbox. Similarly, if you wish, you can direct mail from certain sources direct to a specific folder.

5. Folders

However, I recommend that whilst you set up some folders and, if needed, subfolders, you move mail into them via the Inbox. That way they are less likely to slip your attention, and they can be dragged and dropped into the folders direct from your Inbox. Also, remembering comments earlier about the subconscious brain's discomfort with more than around seven headings, I would advise against having too many main folders.

6. CC Folders

We mentioned earlier how overuse of the "copy" and "copy all" buttons is extremely irritating for many people. One particular folder you may want to consider creating is one for all such emails. You can even set up a specific filter to direct this mail straight to the folder. Either way, you could leave them unread in the folder, saving you time, whilst safe in the knowledge that you know where to find them if need be. After, say a month, you could delete them all. For some people this could be a major time saver.

7. **Files**

Earlier in this Session, there was an example of a filing system for paper files. For electronic files, be they from word processing, spreadsheet, database, graphics or email applications, I have computer files that mirror my paper ones. This consistency makes it a lot easier to find files when you need them and I heartily recommend the idea to you. So, files such as email attachments that need to be kept, can be moved from the Inbox or folder into the appropriate computer file.

8. **Skimming**

In his book *Speed Reading*, Tony Buzan defines skimming as 'that process in which your eye covers certain pre-selected sections in order to gain a **general overview** of that material.' In the paper management section, I advocated an initial skim through the paper mountain to categorise the contents, before then tackling the "Do Now" items. A similar initial skimming method is useful for dealing with large volumes of email. The first skim can be used to identify low-value items, including spam and TUNA, as well as any apparent series of messages (see tip10).

9. **Deleting**

All the low-value items can be deleted immediately without reading. This includes any suspicious emails from unknown addresses, especially if they have attachments. These can be Trojan horses bringing in unwelcome viruses, so if in doubt, delete it out. If you balk at this wholesale deletion approach, reflect on the two opening stories in this section!

10. **Series**

Skimming can often identify series of messages throughout the day relating to the same subject. By reading the last message on the subject, you can often find the initial message and the subsequent responses. The remainder can then be deleted. Cavanagh believes that tips 8, 9 and 10 should not take more than ten minutes and usually reduce the Inbox by around 40%.

11. **Printing**

Please, please, please do not print off **all** your emails. Think of the trees. Be selective. Quickly skim for what should be printed for later reading and what else can be deleted.

12. **Reading**

Skim read the items you print off, flicking through the pages of bulky items. Determine whether it is best to read the item now or at a more convenient time. If you are afraid of forgetting to read something, add it to your "To Do" list, where it will be "in sight and in mind". Alternatively, use the software to flag it or mark it as unread.

13. Previewing

Having considerably slimmed down your Inbox, now is the time to switch to the preview or auto-preview feature. This enables you to see the first few lines of each message. Using this feature all the time makes it harder to obtain that initial overview when you have lots of emails, and may leave you open to viruses and junk mail.

14. Prioritising

Just like your normal "To Do" list, you now need to prioritise your emails. Once again, decide on the eggs (your most important tasks) and do those first. What sequence of priority is the most appropriate for you if you have emails from senior management, internal customers, external customers, projects and your own people?

15. Actioning

Ivy Lee is revisited here as we remind you to complete one email before starting another. As with our earlier discussions on planning and prioritising the day, it is very unproductive to chop and change between emails without fully dealing with them. In summary, by following the recommendations from tips 1 to 15, your email productivity is in grave danger of being greatly increased!

16. Educating

Here it is the Pareto principle which is revisited. Who are the 20% of people sending you 80% of your unwanted emails? Try educating this critical 20%. Explain how you feel about the offending types of emails they send you and why you feel like that. No one can argue with how you feel. You are the world expert. Your aim is to reduce needless cc's and "copy all's", and to take your name off inappropriate distribution or mailing lists.

17. Clearing

As with paper files, your email and other electronic files need periodic clearing out. Sometimes an organisation's server does the job by automatically deleting files after a certain time period. It is a routine task perhaps best done when your energy cycle is low – a rice job between the eggs.

18. Archiving

Depending on your role, you may need to keep some emails for a statutory period for accounting, legal or order-tracking purposes, so check within your organisation. Sometimes emails are automatically archived and thence automatically deleted after set periods. To prevent the deletion of important emails, check your organisation's policy. To be safe, always save such documents to a file on your hard drive.

19. Influencing

If you experience high volumes of incoming email, try and influence senior management to introduce an email audit covering amount and relevance. This can identify the size of the problem and lead to a company policy and usage guidelines. Cavanagh's book provides more details on this and urges organisations to drive email volumes down to a manageable 25 to 30 a day for all employees. You can make a start by using the suggestions above to influence people affecting your own Inbox.

20. Accessing

Various handheld devices, coupled with mobile phones and laptops, provide a growing capability to receive and send emails whilst out of the office. As with email software, it is essential that users make themselves familiar with the mobile technology. It is also essential for work-life balance reasons that users have a policy on their degree of connectivity to the office. Choosing not to access emails after an agreed time of day, for instance, can help that balance.

6. Managing your Outbox

Figure 27 summarises the 20 tips we will now consider.

20 Outbox tips

1. **Exemplary**	11. **Checking**
2. **Purpose**	12. **Fog**
3. **Method**	13. **Tabloids**
4. **Audience**	14. **Flames**
5. **Subject**	15. **Templates**
6. **SCRAPS**	16. **Attachments**
7. **Sentence**	17. **Responding**
8. **Greeting**	18. **Thanking**
9. **Signature**	19. **Out**
10. **Style**	20. **You**

Figure 27

1. Exemplary

A great way to reduce the volume in your Inbox is to be exemplary in your own use of your Outbox. How can you persuade others to reduce their traffic to you, if you yourself are guilty of needless traffic yourself? So be prudent, sparing and selective in your use of cc's, copy all's, For Your Information's and attachments. LOLI is the aim (Less Out = Less In).

2. Purpose

A common phrase in confidential work is "need to know". A suitable phrase for Outbox work is "need to send". Given the drive to reduce needless email, ask yourself 'Do I **really** need to send this email?' 'Do I have a clear purpose?' 'Do I know what I want to achieve?'

3. Method

Even if you do, is email the best option? Review the earlier discussion of the best communication medium to use. Is email the best way of achieving your aim? Note the sign that should be on all PC keyboards – 'Think before you send.'

4. Audience

As with any form of business communication, you should consider and address the needs of your audience. Are you sending this email for your benefit or theirs? What are they likely to know and want to know? Will they understand your jargon?

5. Subject

If your intended audience has a crowded Inbox, your message will be competing for attention with lots of others and will want to avoid the dreaded delete button. In the first rapid scan through (which we discussed earlier), apart from your name, you only have your title to claim attention for your message. The more explanatory and precise this is, therefore, the more chance you have of it being noticed and read. Thus "XYZ PR Agency – Clients' Comments" describes the email's contents much better than a bland heading of "PR".

6. SCRAPS

Have you ever experienced writers' block when trying to compose an email? For those that require more than a brief line or two, the SCRAPS acronym is a tried and tested way of speeding things up. It describes the sequence in which you can write fast emails. It stands for Situation, Complication, Resolution, Action, Politeness, Sentence. Start with the current Situation, going on to any Complications or concerns that you have. Follow on with your recommendation or Resolution of the problem and what Action you want or intend to take. To prevent any fear of abruptness, end with appropriate pleasantries or Politeness.

7. Sentence

The final S of SCRAPS is for Sentence, reminding you to check your opening sentence. As well as your subject heading, does your opening sentence summarise the content? This is important when the preview pane is in use. Newspaper reporters were always taught to do the same in any article they wrote. This was in case it was crowded out by other news, when the sub-editor's pencil would cross out the body of the article, but there might still be room for a succinct first line as a brief news item. Little changes it seems – yesterday's sub-editors are today's delete buttons.

8. Greeting

Immediately before your opening sentence is of course your greeting. An informal, natural style is the norm now, unless the writer does not know the recipient, or the organisation's culture is still formal. However, a golden rule of communication is "to be yourself". If you feel more comfortable with a "Dear Helen" rather than a "Hi" so be it.

9. Signature

It will save you time if you use your software to include your personal contact details and a standard company disclaimer notice from your legal eagles as a signature block at the bottom of each email. Beware of making this too long though. Also, in business environments it is usually best not to include personal quirks such as your current favourite quote or slogan.

10. Style

Email writing style has evolved from its earlier carefree, "anything goes" approach. Earlier views were that spelling, punctuation, grammar and the like did not matter. Well, they do now. Increasingly it seems people take a dim view of these transgressions, which now tend to reflect badly on the sender.

11. Checking

For these reasons, it is imperative that before pressing the send button, you quickly check for spelling, typos and potential misunderstandings. Check too that you are sending it to the right person. There is the cautionary tale of the woman writing a passionate email to her boss only to inadvertently press the "copy all" button. So do check and try to limit your distribution!

12. Fog

Robert Gunning devised a Fog Index on clarity. To check any 100 word plus passage:

- Calculate the average number of words per sentence.
- Calculate the percentage of words with more than two syllables.
- Add the two together and multiply by 0.4.
- Between 8 and 14 is acceptable and between 10 and 12 is recommended.
- Over 14 is heavy, over 18 unreadable, and under 8 childish.
- To achieve the clarity of a 10 to 12 score, as aimed for by some of the Sunday broadsheets, use short words and sentences.
- Is that clear?

13. Tabloids

Talking of newspapers, whilst checking your emails before sending, ensure you would not be embarrassed if they appeared on the front page of a national tabloid. An extreme example is the infamous email from Jo Moore, special adviser to Stephen Byers the then UK Transport Minister, that September 11th was a good day to bury bad news. Your email bloomers may not have such a high profile, yet in this increasingly litigious society, emails are frequently presented as evidence for the prosecution. So this daily tabloid test could save you courting disaster!

14. Flames

'A vitriolic or abusive email, typically one sent in quick response to another message' is the dictionary definition of this term. You can see how a similar riposte could quickly lead to flame warfare. Such emails would certainly not pass the tabloid test. Psychologist Dr David Lewis is quoted as saying that 'Flames are often the response of stressed managers working against impossible deadlines, which in the past would have been dealt with by talking to the offender. These days, time pressures lead some bosses to use flames by email instead.' Sometimes they copy others, adding shame to flame. So to save you embarrassment, the next time you receive an email you do not like and are tempted to retort in kind – desist. Sleep on it and send a more measured response the following day. This will save you the damaging fallout that warfare usually brings to both parties. Remember the Chinese proverb – 'Before seeking revenge, dig two graves.'

15. Templates

If you send out standard requests or responses to requests, you might save some time by establishing templates of standard email letters or forms. The software will normally guide you through this and help you design tailored templates for repeated use.

16. Attachments

There is a tendency to send too many attachments with more detail and more graphics than the recipient needs. They take time to download, more time to read, and can create exasperation and a poor image of the sender if they are not absolutely essential. As with the new spam legislation, a better option might sometimes be to have people "opt in" to receive them if they want. For instance, I recently received an attachment of a four-page summary of a major report, with the offer of the full report if I wanted it. The sender certainly earned brownie points from me!

17. Responding

Research suggests that two thirds of emails need a response, but fewer than one in five people can now respond the same day. So do not feel guilty if you are in the vast majority who can't. Also, before responding, be sure that you need to.

18. Thanking

One area where responses are often no longer needed is the 'thank you for your email', which often led to 'thank you for your thank you' or similar. This was fine in the earlier, low-volume days, but today can clog up busy people's Inboxes. So, if you really want to acknowledge something, before you send the email consider whether a telephone call or mention at your next meeting might be better.

19. Out

The "out of office" function on your software can be used to inform people that you are out of the office until a specific date. If the matter is urgent you can direct them to alternative contacts. This can help prevent customers or colleagues getting annoyed, particularly if they were expecting a quick response from you. Also, it usually reduces the amount of emails waiting for you on your return. However, beware of leaving "out of office" promises you cannot deliver. One such automatic response I received to a query spoke of a desire for superior service. Despite a reminder of the query, I am still waiting for the reply! So make sure you deliver what you promise, out of the office or in.

20. You

During this Session you will have seen how email can be a great time saver or time waster. There is a need to manage email to reduce excess volumes coming in and going out and deal speedily and effectively with what is left. The rewards for you and your organisation are more time for the important things, less waste and less stress. The more you can influence others to follow suit, the more will be gained – not least by you.

Summary

The way you manage your Inbox and Outbox will paint a picture of you to your seniors, peers, customers and other work colleagues. Applying the above ideas will help you to be seen as a considerate sender and accomplished receiver of emails. Intention is not the same as action though. You are, therefore, invited to review the contents of this section and draw up your own action plan.

Email Action Plan

Tick the ideas you intend implementing immediately. Add others once these are actioned.

Inbox Tips				Outbox Tips			
1.	Guidelines	11.	Printing	1.	Exemplary	11.	Checking
2.	Checking	12.	Reading	2.	Purpose	12.	Fog
3.	Software	13.	Previewing	3.	Method	13.	Tabloids
4.	Filters	14.	Prioritising	4.	Audience	14.	Flames
5.	Folders	15.	Actioning	5.	Subject	15.	Templates
6.	Cc folders	16.	Educating	6.	SCRAPS	16.	Attachments
7.	Files	17.	Clearing	7.	Sentence	17.	Responding
8.	Skimming	18.	Archiving	8.	Greeting	18.	Thanking
9.	Deleting	19.	Influencing	9.	Signature	19.	Out
10.	Series	20.	Accessing	10.	Style	20.	You

7. Faster report writing

Books such as John Bowden's Writing A Report (see bibliography) should be sought for detailed advice on this subject. However, here are three quick tips on saving time on your report writing. First though, an exercise...

The Alphabet Exercise

Try this out on one or two unsuspecting souls. The rules are:

- They must not see the questions or answers.
- They must do it in their heads.
- No writing anything down.
- Ask them the question and give them as much time as they want to think.
- Just ask them how sure they are of their answers.

1. How many two-letter combinations of two different letters can you think of using the two letters A and B?

2. How many two-letter combinations of two different letters can you think of using the three letters A, B and C?

3. How many two-letter combinations of two different letters can you think of using the four letters A, B, C and D?

The answers are:

1.	Two: AB, BA	2.	Six:	AB, AC	3.	Twelve:	AB, AC, AD
				BA, BC			BA, BC, BD
				CA, CB			CA, CB, CD
							DA, DB, DC

Usually people struggle with this exercise. The reason is they cannot write it down. Once written down, the solution is obvious.

This has implications for report writing. Often people try to write reports from their head. If they cannot even juggle four well-known letters easily, how can they juggle the many more ideas and concepts they have in mind to include in their report?

The answer is to "brain dump". That means getting a blank sheet of paper and simply scribbling down as fast as you can anything you can think of about the subject. Do not worry about order, logic, or whether you will eventually include it. You will have plenty of time for that afterwards. It is a one person version of brainstorming, where it is quantity of ideas you want at this stage, without any judgmental sifting and sorting.

Once you have all these random ideas on the page to look at, the brain can come up with suitable report headings under which most, if not all, of the ideas will comfortably sit. Re-jig the sequence and you have the outline of the report. This is half the work done. Writing the report then becomes a much quicker and easier matter. Try and do all this in your head in a logical "batting order" and it will take you forever. It is the dumping of your thoughts onto paper that is the key. The same principles apply to writing a training course, writing a proposal or writing a book.

A variant of the linear "brain dump" is the "mind map" or "spider drawing". Pioneered by Tony Buzan, mind maps can save time in meeting minute taking and in personal study, as well as writing reports (see the bibliography).

Finally, a third time-saving option is becoming increasingly common. That is the use of paper copies of PowerPoint type slides for presentations, perhaps with some supporting appendices for those who might want more detail. Provided this is well prepared and presented with the recipients' needs in mind, it can be a very acceptable alternative to a formal written report. It can be enhanced by a brief one or at most two-page executive summary, which is a recommended feature of most types of reports.

SUMMARY OF SESSION SIX: Paperwork And The Modern Office

1. Choose the paper and electronic time toolkit combination that suits you best.
2. Use a paperwork organiser and wastepaper bin to keep a clear, stress-free desk and reduce your paper mountain to a manageable molehill.
3. If you cannot file and retrieve documents quickly and consistently, revamp your files and have a "Bin Bag Day".
4. Ensure you profitably use, not wastefully abuse, your email, or it will cost you time and your organisation money.
5. Use the 20 tips to reduce your Inbox to a manageable size and encourage awareness and action if email is an organisational hindrance not a help.
6. Lead by setting a good example with your Outbox and implement your own email action plan.
7. Use brain dumping, mind mapping or bullet-point slide summaries to outline and write better and faster reports.

Session

7

Session Seven: Personal Action Plan

So here comes the hard part. After recapping what we have covered, you are asked to draw up a detailed action plan to help you apply what you have learnt. The Session covers:

1. Review 1 – stress reduction exercise.
2. Review 2 – your personal action plan.
3. The supporting cast.
4. Measuring your progress.
5. Continuing your improvement.

1. Review 1 – stress reduction exercise

Skim through the Session summaries below. As you do so, tick the ideas that can help you reduce stress. The number of stress reducers applicable to you will depend partly upon whether you have people reporting to you. Make a note of the number of ticks at the end to highlight the many ways you can take action to reduce stress at work.

SUMMARY OF SESSION ONE: Principles

1. Manage the day, don't let the day manage you.
2. Accept the need to change your time management. **'If you always do what you've always done, you'll always get what you've always got.'**
3. Unblock your learning by tackling any personal, psychological or organisational barriers.
4. Know your innate time management strengths and weaknesses and work on both.
5. Beware of defective mindsets, such as the Don Quixote Syndrome, Parkinson's Law and Faulty Time Norms.
6. Decide what is **really important** in your life and be prepared to pay the price.
7. Keep balancing any short-term and long-term work-life imbalances and managing-doing imbalances.

SUMMARY OF SESSION TWO: Planning Ahead

1. To plan and prioritise effectively, you need clarity about your role and what is expected of you.
2. Determine the Key Result Areas of your job and look for opportunities to improve each one.
3. Agree SMARTER objectives to reach a consensus about exactly what you are trying to achieve.

4.   Start-line-focused Action Plans spread the workload, improve work quality, reduce stress and provide a simple way of monitoring results.

5.   Plan time in your diary for your personal projects and objectives as well as those of other people, using the "you" time squiggle or electronic diary blocking techniques.

6.   Schedule a maximum of two major deadlines per week, bringing work forward to avoid conflicts if necessary. Set realistic time scales, which allow for "real world" situations.

7.   Planning without controlling is a waste of time. But keep controls simple, appropriate for the person and the task, and visible – in sight and in mind.

8.   Good time management ideas can be used at home as well as work.

SUMMARY OF SESSION THREE: Planning The Day

1.   Write a daily "To Do" list. Start on the most important task first and complete each task before you go on to the next.

2.   Prioritise tasks and do not let the **urgent** squeeze out the **important.**

3.   Keep your important monthly objectives and milestones on a visible separate list and include them in your daily planning during the month.

4.   Do not over-plan and be sure to expect the unexpected.

5.   Plan and look for opportunities to use committed time productively.

6.   Ideally, plan the day the night before, and write down all tasks, including personal ones, in one place.

7.   Be both **efficient** and **effective** by focusing on the 20% of work that will give you 80% of your results.

SUMMARY OF SESSION FOUR: Personal Time

1.   You will achieve most of your key results when you are working by yourself. Block this time in your diary to work on your priorities for each day.

2.   Safeguard these blocks of "you" time with Red Time and other techniques.

3.   Learn to say "No" in an acceptable way to prevent yourself becoming overloaded.

4.   Be assertive rather than aggressive or passive, treating everyone with respect and earning the respect and co-operation of others in the process.

5.   Save time by carefully analysing the real problem, before writing an objective, generating options and implementing a plan.

6.   Safeguard your health by choosing not to be stressed, using good time management techniques, and promoting an organisational Work-Life Balance culture.

7.   Reduce any tendencies to procrastinate by having clear goals and priorities, macro and micro action plans, fewer interruptions, less workload, less clutter, less negative self-talk and mind mapped reports.

SUMMARY OF SESSION FIVE: People Time

1. Develop a professional working relationship with your boss, mindful that you will always have three options if you are unhappy with this.
2. Good bosses get results from their people by directing, developing and motivating them by AGREEMENT.
3. Multiply your time by improving your delegation skills when you give and receive delegated tasks using the TIARA acronym.
4. Suggest a Meetings Charter to save time, improve their quality, and increase commitment to decisions made at them.
5. Improve communications by "managing the boundaries" with other parts of the organisation to reduce the dangers of crisis management and constantly changed priorities
6. Maximise the return on your time management training by training early, training modern, being supportive and following up.

SUMMARY OF SESSION SIX: Paperwork And The Modern Office

1. Choose the paper and electronic time toolkit combination that suits you best.
2. Use a paperwork organiser and wastepaper bin to keep a clear, stress-free desk and reduce your paper mountain to a manageable molehill.
3. If you cannot file and retrieve documents quickly and consistently, revamp your files and have a "Bin Bag Day".
4. Ensure you profitably use, not wastefully abuse, your email, or it will cost you time and your organisation money.
5. Use the 20 tips to reduce your Inbox to a manageable size and encourage awareness and action if email is an organisational hindrance not a help.
6. Lead by setting a good example with your Outbox and implement your own email action plan.
7. Use brain dumping, mind mapping or bullet-point slide summaries to outline and write better and faster reports.

Total number of ideas that can help to reduce stress: _____

2. Review 2 – your personal action plan

As was said in Session One, 'If you always do what you've always done, you'll always get what you've always got.' Therefore, for you to improve your time management, you will need to do some things differently, try new ideas, and change the status quo. It is now time for you to change these words into deeds.

From the above six Session summaries, what are you going to do differently to what you do at present? What are you going to do more of, less of, stop doing and start doing? When do you intend making a start on each of these?

> From the six Session summaries, what are you going to do differently to what you do at present? What are you going to do more of, less of, stop doing and start doing? When do you intend making a start on each of these?

Might I suggest that you implement the easiest ideas first. Get some "quick wins" and then review your list and start tackling the other ideas during the next few weeks. Remembering that to fail to prepare is to prepare to fail, you are now ready to succeed by preparing your personal improvement plan on the next page.

3. The supporting cast

At work, who has a vested interest in your being productive and effective? Is it not your immediate boss? This might be an ideal opportunity to book a meeting with them to discuss what you have learnt, what you want to do differently, and what support you might need from them.

As well as the perceived benefits to you, talk about the benefits for them if you are able to be more productive, less stressed and have a better work-life balance. Spell out the specific help you need from them in order to give them the benefit of the "new you". This might involve agreeing how you can create some uninterrupted time, clarifying some aspects of what is expected of you, discussing the benefits of earlier delegation, changing email practices and so on. I also suggest that you involve your boss in measuring your time management improvements (which we cover next).

At home, if there is a significant other, or supportive friends, why not have a similar discussion with them. Focus on how you might do better at work and enjoy a better quality of life outside work.

Personal Improvement Plan

What I am going to do	My timing (start/finish)

4. Measuring your progress

It is possible for you to measure your improvement using the methods adopted in the time management training research study mentioned elsewhere in this book. This involves:

- Agreeing the time management key skills you need.
- Assessing your effectiveness now and in the future.
- Checking this out with a knowledgeable third party.

Your time management key skills

The list of key skills offered here is shown in the exercise below. It was used on 11 of the 19 courses surveyed. The other courses had slight variations. For instance, for some sales teams, delegation and interruptions were not relevant, whereas making effective journey plans and achieving monthly objectives were. I therefore suggest that you tick the key skills relevant to you, delete those that are not relevant, and add any others that are.

Key Skills Measurement Exercise

Time Management Key Skill	Column 1 Relevance to me ✓	Column 2 Current rating (1 low to 7 high)	Column 3 3 month rating (1 low to 7 high)
Date ⇨			
1. Effectively plan, prioritise and schedule each day.			
2. Achieve better results by working on the important as well as the urgent.			
3. Manage interruptions and create quality time for quality tasks.			
4. Link medium-term goals with daily plans.			
5. Improve management of the desk, email, paperwork, telephone and the modern office.			
6. Delegate but don't abdicate, to free up more personal time and develop others.			
7. Chair and/or contribute to more effective meetings.			
8. Manage personal health and reduce time management-related stress.			

Time Management Key Skill	Column 1 Relevance to me ✓	Column 2 Current rating (1 low to 7 high)	Column 3 3 month rating (1 low to 7 high)
Date ⇨			
9. Set and achieve clear objectives through action planning and reviewing.			
10. Reduce the risk of forgetting things and not following up.			
11. Learn to say "No" in a non career-threatening, assertive way.			
12. Overcome procrastination by working on tasks in priority order.			
13. Improve the work/home balance.			
14. Know what is **really** important to you in both your business and your private life.			
15. Positively influence the time culture of your organisation.			
Total score		(A)	(B)

Assessing your improved effectiveness

Against each of your key time management skills, rate yourself on a scale of 1 (low or poor) to 7 (high or good). Base your rating on your perceived skill level before you started reading the book. Repeat the exercise in about three months time, after you have had a chance to implement some of the ideas.

Rather than become excited about statistical nuances, for this exercise, let us keep it simple. The procedure to measure your improvement is as follows:

1. Total your assessment scores in Column 2 (current rating). Call this total A.
2. Total your assessment scores in Column 3 (later rating). Call this total B.
3. Subtract A from B to give your score. Call this figure C.
4. For your percentage improvement, divide C by A and multiply by 100.

Assessing your assessment

The academic fraternity are not too impressed by your views alone. They like a second opinion. This could be the boss, a colleague, a friend, or someone who sees you operating on a regular basis.

So why not engage the support of one such person, show them your scores, and ask them to tick one of these boxes:

I agree ❏ I tend to agree ❏ I am not sure ❏ I tend to disagree ❏ I disagree ❏

It may also be interesting to obtain examples of your changed or unchanged behaviour to support their assessment.

In the research, we found that 95% of managers either agreed or tended to agree with the figures. If you have a different experience, this could be a very helpful "reality check". Talk through any reasons for the different views if they exist and learn from the feedback.

5. Continuing your improvement

Congratulations on the new ideas and techniques on time management that you now know. Yet as Goethe once said, 'Knowing is not enough. We must apply. Willing is not enough. We must do.' So good luck as you apply your new knowledge and practise the new techniques. As was found in the clasping and unclasping of hands exercise, it might feel awkward and difficult at first. Persevere and the awkwardness will go and you will reap the benefits.

> 'Knowing is not enough.
> We must apply.
> Willing is not enough.
> We must do.'
>
> Goethe

However, as most writers agree, time management is not a one-off learning experience. It is a topic that will repay regular refresher visits. So when you have absorbed your set of new-found skills, keep looking for further improvements you can make. Your rationale is provided by management guru Peter Drucker in his seminal work *The Effective Executive.*

Everything requires time. It is the one truly universal condition. All work takes place in time and uses up time. Yet most people take for granted this unique, irreplaceable, and necessary resource. Nothing else, perhaps, distinguishes effective executives as much as their tender loving care of time.

> Nothing else, perhaps, distinguishes effective executives as much as their tender loving care of time.
>
> Peter Drucker,
>
> The Effective Executive

Drucker also goes on to say that man is ill equipped to manage his time. However, after having read this book, I hope you now feel much better equipped to provide the tender loving care to manage your time more effectively in the pursuit of your work and life goals. Love every minute!

Bibliography

Bibliography

Adair, John (1987) *How To Manage Your Time.* Guildford: Talbot-Adair.

Allen, David (2001) *Getting Things Done: How To Achieve Stress-Free Productivity.* London: Piatkus.

Beck, Ken and Beck, Kate (1982) *Assertiveness at Work.* Maidenhead: McGraw-Hill.

Belbin, Meredith (2003) *Management Teams: Why They Succeed or Fail* (2nd edn.). Oxford: Heinemann.

Blanchard, Kenneth, Onchan Jnr, William and Burrows, Hal (1994) *The One Minute Manager Meets the Monkey.* New York: Harper Collins.

Bowden, John (2004) *Writing A Report: How To Prepare, Write And Present Effective Reports.* Oxford: How To Books.

Buzan, Tony (1982) *Use Your Head.* London: BBC Books.

Buzan, Tony (1997) *Speed Reading.* London: BBC Books.

Cavanagh, Christina (2003) *Managing Your E-Mail: Thinking Outside The Inbox.* Hoboken NJ: John Wiley.

Covey, Stephen, Merrill, Roger, Merril, Rebecca (1994) *First Things First.* New York: Simon & Schuster.

Davidson, Mike (1995) *The Grand Strategist.* London: McMillan

DfEE (2000) *Work-Life Balance 2000 Baseline Survey.* London: Department for Education and Employment.

Drucker, Peter (1970) *The Effective Executive.* London: Pan Books.

DTI (2001) *Work-Life Balance: The Business case.* London: Department of Trade and Industry.

Fiore, Neil (1989) *The Now Habit: A Strategic Program for Overcoming Procrastination and Enjoying Guilt-Free Play.* New York: Tarcher/Putnam.

Garnet, Andy (1993) *It's About Time – Working Time Survey.* London: Industrial Society.

Gleeson, Kerry (2000) *The Personal Efficiency Program* (3rd edn.). New York: Wiley.

Green, Peter (2002) *Does Time Management Training Work? An Evaluation.* Oxford: Oxford Brookes Business School.

Kirkpatrick, Donald (1994) *Evaluating Training Programmes: The Four Levels.* New York: McGraw Hill.

Lakein, Alan (1973) *How To Get Control Of Your Time and Your Life.* New York: Signet.

Mackenzie, Alec (1997) *The Time Trap.* (3rd edn.) New York: AMACOM.

Noe, R. (1986) *'Trainees' attributes and attitudes: neglected influences in training effectiveness',* Academy of Management Review, Vol. 11, No. 4, pp.736-749.

Noon, James (1998) *Start Time Forward.* Burgess Hill: Filofax.

Oncken Jr., William and Wass, Donald (1974) *'Who's got the monkey?' Harvard Business Review. Nov/Dec.* Harvard: Harvard Business School.

Roger, Derek (2002) *Managing Stress: Live Long and Prosper* (2nd edn.). Cookham: CIM.

Schein, Edgar H. (1988) *Process Consultation: Its Role in Organization Development, Vol.1.* Reading MA.: Addison-Wesley.

Starr, Julie (2003) *The Coaching Manual: The Definitive Guide To The Process, Principles And Skills Of Personal Coaching.* London: Prentice Hall.

Treacy, Declan (1991) *Clear Your Desk.* London: Century Business.

Wheatley, Ruth (2000) *Taking The Strain: A survey of managers and workplace stress.* London: The Chartered Management Institute.

Index

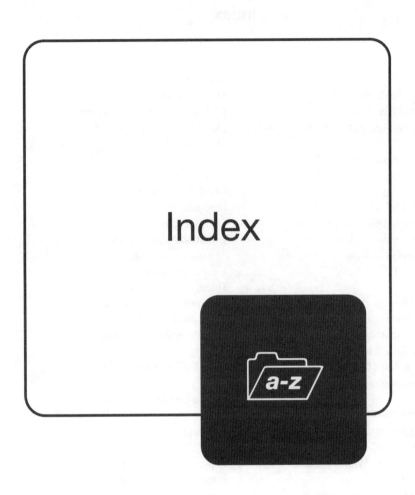

Index

Notes

ƒILOFAX®

The Managing Time Workshop
Research-proven training that works

Workshop aim
To enable managers, specialists and support staff at all levels of experience to organise their time more effectively.

Workshop objectives
To enable participants to:
- Plan and prioritise in a changing world.
- Link medium-term plans to daily plans.
- Control interruptions and overcome procrastination.
- Solve problems and hit deadlines with less stress.
- Manage and integrate paper and emails.
- Improve meetings, delegation and work-life balance.
- Have a personal action plan.

What the seminar will cover

Principles
The Chicken Farmer Syndrome; unblocking your learning; Don Quixote, time traps and other hazards; deciding what is important and balancing the imbalances.

Planning Ahead
The Vision-to-Action cycle; solving problems and setting objectives; start-line-focused plans and projects; diary management and the cure for "cancellitis"; scheduling and monitoring that hits deadlines.

Planning and Prioritising the Day
Flexible planning and prioritising amidst change; achieving the important, value-adding tasks, as well as the urgent; effective use of committed time.

Personal Time
Planning and protecting quality time for quality tasks; managing interruptions; saying "No" and being assertive; managing personal health and stress; overcoming procrastination.

People Time
Getting the best from your boss and your people; delegating without abdicating; better group and one-to-one meetings; high-tech meetings versus travel; crisis management, boundary management and better communication skills; ensuring more ROT (Return On Training).

Paper and Electronic Mail
Choosing your time management toolkit; how to manage your desk and clear the paper mountain; file management; linking PCs and networks to paper-based systems; the use and abuse of email; managing the In and Outboxes; writing faster and better reports.

Personal Action Plan
Summary of the 100 plus time management tips and techniques; implementation checklist; progress review tool; personal improvement measure.

Designed to organise

Time is costly to organisations and precious to individuals. Yet the reality for many is wasted time at work and too little time for life.

For over 80 years, Filofax, the world's leader in personal productivity, has pioneered tools and techniques to help you make the most of your time. Filofax personal organisers have become a way of life for millions of people even in today's high-tech world. Indeed, as this book goes to print, Filofax sold more personal organisers last year than during any other year in its rich history.

A recent research study found that people provided with Filofax organisers as part of their time management training improved more than those without one. The Filofax Professional System is therefore the perfect tool to enable you to harness the 100 plus ideas and techniques in Peter Green's *Managing Time* book. This unique planning system puts you in control, enabling you to organise yourself quickly and easily – you'll never find a better investment!

Research-proven training

Filofax conduct regular open time management workshops in partnership with the CIM. We can also arrange in-company time management training events designed for the specific needs of your organisation. Both are based on this *Managing Time* book, which describes the independent research on its proven effectiveness.

Contact

For your personal copy of our latest product and service catalogue:
Tel. 0990 502230
www.filofax.co.uk

For details of our open and in-company
Time management workshops:
Tel: 01444 238144
Fax: 01444 238 119
Email: timeman@filofax.co.uk

For time management workshop content, see the previous page.